MW01289628

ENJOY THE DECLINE

To Dirty Harriet, Zoey, and Oscar

TABLE OF CONTENTS

Chapter 1   Psychological Adaptation   6

Chapter 2   The New Economic Reality   27

Chapter 3   The Art of Minimalism   57

Chapter 4   Mortal   75

Chapter 5   Family and Friends   87

Chapter 6   Career and Education   115

Chapter 7   Finance and Investing   124

Chapter 8   Plunder   141

Chapter 9   SHTF   153

Chapter 10   Fight or Flight   164

Chapter 11   Revenge   178

CAVEAT

In intellectual honesty I have to warn the reader that though "Enjoy the Decline" was meant to be an uplifting book, parts of it are incredibly depressing, if not, outright debilitating. This was not meant to depress the reader, but was rather a required and natural consequence of having to speak candidly and truthfully about the economic and political condition of the United States. Therefore, I strongly recommend reading no more than one chapter at a time, specifically the chapters in Part I, as those are the chapters that are particularly depressing.

Additionally, regular readers of Captain Capitalism may wish to skip Chapter 2 – "The New Economic Reality"- in that it is merely a review of the economic condition of the United States. This isn't to say it wouldn't be a good refresher course in economics or that you wouldn't enjoy it, but it is largely intended for new readers unfamiliar with some basic economic concepts and statistics.

It is my sincere wish that this book proves useful to you and provides everybody with the necessary hope and know-how to "Enjoy the Decline."

PREFACE

Any doubt about the future of the United States and the direction the country was heading was quickly eliminated in the election of 2012. Most of us were hoping the first four years of the Obama administration was a fluke in American history. That his election was only possible because of a childlike naivety on the part of an ignorant electorate. That the voting public, temporarily star-struck, opted to vote with their emotions and not their heads. And that after four years of the worst economic performance of any president since FDR, people would wake up, grow up, realize the error of their ways, and vote like mature adults the next time around.

Unfortunately most of us were wrong.

With the election of 2012 the American people have made it very clear which path they wish to take the United States down – socialism. Whether cognizant of this fact or completely ignorant about it, it doesn't matter, people voted the way they did. They could still be fawning over President Obama like a teenage girl or Chris Matthews. They could be the typical voter who votes for socialism because it sounds "nice." They could be the galactically ignorant soccer mom who believes no amount of other people's money is too good for her children. Or they could be fully informed socialists knowing damn well what they're doing confiscating other people's money. The reason why doesn't matter, all that matters "is what is."

Of course "is what is" is a devastating blow to lot of conservatives, libertarians, freedom-lovers and what I henceforth refer to as "Real Americans." Not just because politically or ideologically "our team lost," but because our entire lives and all of our futures are now in question.

Understand that you, me and everybody else who loved America, believed in America, and loves freedom grew up under some basic assumptions. And not only did we grow up under these basic

3

assumptions, we based our lives and our decisions around these premises. We assumed the United States would continue to be the freest country in the world. We assumed we would be able to keep the lion's share of our income and wealth. We assumed hard work, innovation, and efficiency would be rewarded. We assumed if we worked hard at something our dreams could be realized. In short it was all that made America not just great, but the most successful country in the history of the world and we poured our hearts and souls into these beliefs.

Unfortunately, with these basic premises no longer certain all of the work, effort and time we put into our lives, and therefore our futures, are also no longer certain. Did you attend college to become a doctor? Well too bad, you may have wage controls with Obamacare. Did you work hard to become an engineer and create something? Too bad, we may have to confiscate your income at a 60% level. Did you have dreams of starting up a motorcycle shop? Too bad we're going to regulate and tax it out of existence. Were you planning on marrying a nice girl? Too bad, feminism has destroyed the quality of women. Did you want to have children? Too bad the state will raise your children. Did you want your children to have a better life than you? Too bad, your generational peers voted to mortgage your children into financial slavery. Say, nice sizeable 401k plan you have there! Too bad, we're going to nationalize it just like Argentina did.

The end result is EXTRAORDINARILY depressing. Not only is it increasingly likely you've lived your life in vain, but you've lived a significant percentage of your life in slavery. Worse still any dreams you had are becoming rapidly impossible. And even worse than that is without your dreams there's nothing you can uniquely achieve that would define you.

In short your life has no meaning.

This epiphany, whether consciously realized or not, obviously takes a devastating toll on all Real Americans. Anecdotal though it may be, everyone I personally know is more depressed today than they were a decade ago. I know more than one rugged individualist contemplating suicide. And there's no shortage of old men I know who MEAN IT when they say,

"Thank god I'm not going to be around to see this country collapse!"

The entire population of Real Americans is defeated emotionally, psychologically and spiritually. With no purpose or future they are simply asking "Why go on? Why continue? Why did I work so hard? What is left to live for?"

But dire as the situation may be, there is some hope. *Genuine* hope, not the hope that is found in presidential speeches and pablum. Hope that is practical, real, and will yield results. However, this hope comes from the only place real hope can come from – within – which means we have to focus on ourselves and what is within our control to realize this hope and capitalize on it. This isn't to say that the world will turn out all roses and dachshunds, nor is it going to be the "faux depressing type of hope" akin to when your mother would say,

"Well at least you aren't a cancerous, Ebola-infected, starving, blind quadriplegic, leper living in war-torn Ethiopia with lice!"

But at minimum this book will show you there *is* a future, you *can* live a happy life, the left *will* get their comeuppance, and no matter how bad it gets, there is always a way to "Enjoy the Decline."

CHAPTER 1
PSYCHOLOGICAL ADAPTATION

"Let us eat and drink for tomorrow we die."
-Ephesians

Berlin 1945

Too tired to play video games, but not tired enough to fall asleep, I found myself watching The History Channel late one wintery night in Casper, Wyoming. I managed to finish two episodes of "Pawn Stars," before the programming switched to a WWII documentary. I debated turning it off and going to bed, but glad I didn't' because it proved to be one of the most interesting, but dark documentaries I've ever seen.

Specifically, it was about civilian life in Berlin while under the siege of the Russians in 1945. Berlin was nothing but rubble, supply lines were shot, and life for the average Berliner was wretched. They couldn't escape to the east in fear the Russians would kill or rape them (or both). And they couldn't escape to the west, not out of fear that the Americans and Brits would do the same, but that the Gestapo would kill them. This left them trapped in a city that not only couldn't support the population, but a city that would become their grave. To survive they resorted to desperate acts. They ate horses, leather from furniture and whatever else they could find. And if this wasn't enough it was all under the maddening backdrop of constant Soviet shelling. It was arguably some of the most miserable living conditions humans had ever suffered.

But where the documentary took a particularly dark turn was when it started showing footage of Berliners throwing parties in the midst of this hell. I didn't understand it at first until the narrator explained since these people were doomed, they logically came to the macabre conclusion they might as well live it up while they could. Such "maniacal levity" was also documented by Albert Speer in his book "Inside the Third Reich" as he witnessed people being irrationally happy and cheerful even though their demise was imminent. The documentary became even more morose when a lot of these parties ended up becoming "suicide parties" where the participants would break out the hidden booze, whoop it up one last final time, and then all commit suicide at the end of the evening.

Of course the theme of the documentary did nothing for my sleep, but making it worse was that all these videos were visually dark and poorly lit. Since the city was constantly being shelled, there was no electricity. This left bonfires as the primary source of light and gave the videos a particularly eerie and barbaric feel as you saw people mix in and out of the shadows, all laughing maniacally. Booze would flow, people would laugh, glasses would break, participants would fall over one another, but it was as if the party was being held at the Arkham Asylum. They were no longer humans, they were turning into animals. They were no longer sane.

Or were they?

For it's one thing to lay there, comfortably on a futon with a full meal and a shot of Rumpie in your stomach and do some Monday morning quarterbacking 67 years after the fact. It's another thing to have lived it and experienced it.   And while we enjoy the luxury of warmth, food, security and safety, the besieged Berliners of 1945 had no such luxuries.

Were their actions dark?

Yes.

Were their actions morose?

Most certainly.

Were their actions macabre?

Absolutely.

But they were also 100% completely logical, sane and right in doing what they did.

Bad as it was, dire and futile as it was, they were still about their wits. They had no option to flee, they had no option to fight, so what else were they supposed to do? Their only other option was to enjoy what little time they had left. If anything it is a testament to the optimism of humankind and the resilience of the human mind. Even in the darkest pits of hell, people still did what they could to enjoy it. And it is here that we need to pull a lesson from the besieged Berliners because if there is an example of enjoying the decline (although an incredibly EXTREME example), occupied Berlin and its "last hurrah parties" are it.

Naturally the plight of citizens in 1945 Berlin is not perfectly analogous to the plight of Real Americans in 2012. We do not have the Russians at the outskirts of town waiting to slaughter us. We do not have a secret state police hanging us if we're caught trying to escape. We have food, clothing, shelter, safety and freedoms that simply do not compare to 1945 Berlin. However, we do share four key things in common:

1. A environment that has changed on us rendering our previous plans impotent
2. A situation we are powerless to control
3. A situation that requires we change our psychology to understand it
4. A situation that requires we change our behavior in order to make the best of it

In short, we must do what the besieged Berliners did in 1945 - change our psychologies allowing us to not just adapt to our new environment, but maximize the pleasure we can gain from it. For achieving a similar such psychological adaptation is key to not just maximizing what life we have left, but enjoying the decline in the United States today.

Letting Go of the United States

The first psychological adaptation or "epiphany" you need to have is arguably the hardest – you need to let go of the United States.

If there was ever a country to love, it was the United States. With its glorious and unrivalled history, as well as all the good it has done throughout the world, as well as all the promises it has given her people, no country in the history of the world even comes close. It is the single best thing to happen to all of humankind, ever, period. If the United States were to be in female form it would be a combination of Jennifer Aniston, a young Ann Margret, a young Sophia Loren with a splash of sassy Katherine Hepburn and a touch of naughty Bettie Page. It will never be repeated or even rivaled. Therefore it is the hardest thing for any Real American to watch the United States slowly get beaten to death.

Whether you'd like to admit it or not, the United States is in terminal decline. Making it even worse, is its inevitable demise will not be at the hands of a stronger foreign force, but rather at the hands of its own unfathomably ignorant citizens brainwashed and duped by its own unfathomably evil citizens. It is an internal cancer that is eating away at our beloved nation and despite our best efforts it is spreading.

It is here we have to realize that the United States, no matter how much we love her, is no different than a loved one or a family member. She is finite, she has a life cycle, and like all empires in the history of empires, she too will fail and die. The issue is whether we can accept this or not for our own mental health. Just like dealing with a dying family member, there comes the point in time that we have to admit the inevitable and let go. Not for the sake of the dying, but for our own mental sake. If we can't accept this reality, the only people we hurt are ourselves. Of course this doesn't mean we don't do what we can to hopefully bring our loved ones back, but at the same time we cannot be delusional about it.

We must also realize that, for better or worse, the United States is a democracy and this is what the people wanted. Opposing it would not only be against the principles of the United States, but it would also be the definition of tyranny. This should provide you some solace, or at least assuage any guilt you have, in that you were not responsible for the demise of this country. You did what you could. You did your best. You voted, you were politically active, you tried to convince people to vote for freedom, you lived up to your civic responsibility. That's all anybody can do. The rest of it is outside of your control because this is a democracy regardless of how ignorant the electorate.

Finally, we have to admit that the country is changing.

In the movie "I Am Legend" Will Smith plays a post-apocalyptic scientist trying to find a cure for a disease that infects humans and turns them into zombies. He has no human contact, and only his dog for companionship. In one of the sadder scenes his dog gets infected and starts to become a zombie itself. Tortured by the fact he knows what he has to do, Smith's character caresses the dog, hugs it one last time, and proceeds to break its neck. We must also come to this same realization.

Soon the body that lay before us will no longer be the strongest most successful nation we all grew up with and loved. It will be nothing more than a pile of cancerous cells resulting in a completely different, vastly inferior, and (most likely) more hostile country. It is here you must let go of and divorce yourself from the United States. Not because we don't love her, but because as a country she no longer represents the freedom, liberty and happiness she once did. She will become a completely different being.

There is good news, however.

While we may mourn the loss of the United States, America will continue on forever. The reason why is the United States is a country. A physical location. A plot of dirt and water defined by imaginary lines denoting its borders. There is nothing inherently special about the physical United States. It is the people, the ideas, and above all else the concept of America that has made this land great. In other words, just as you don't love a person for their elbows, their toenails or their hair, but rather their personality, so too do you not love a country for its physical traits, but rather what it stands for and the opportunity it provides. So no matter how many socialists they vote in and no matter how many taxes are passed, America will never die because it is an idea. It is an ideal. It is a law of human nature that free people, allowed to pursue their dreams and keep the vast majority of their wealth will ALWAYS, ALWAYS, ALWAYS be a greater people and form a greater country than any other form of government. And just as you cannot kill the Law of Gravity, so too can you not kill the Law of America. America will live on forever.

1 in 300,000,000

Another psychological adjustment you must make in order to enjoy the decline is to realize what you do and do not control. Quintillions of calories of energy are spent every year by Americans worrying, fretting, and concerning themselves over things they simply do not control. For example I sit in amazement every year watching Minnesota Vikings fans build themselves into seizures as they see the abysmal performance, year after year

...after year

...after year

of the Minnesota Vikings:

The cursing, the swearing, the cheering, THE TOUCHDOWN.......the flag, the reviewing, the penalties, the *REVERSAL OF THE TOUCHDOWN*, the

MORE ANGRY CURSING, the THROWING-OF-THE-REMOTE, and even the full-grown-man-crying.

All because a bunch of guys WHO THE FANS HAVE NOTHING TO DO WITH, HAVE NEVER MET, AND HAVE NO PERSONAL RELATION WITH threw a funny looking ball badly and didn't run good enough!

The reason we can all laugh is because ultimately one group of large men throwing the funny looking ball better than another group of large men really has no material effect on us or our lives. However, the trick to realizing what you do and do not control becomes much more difficult when it's over something that DOES affect you. The weather, the stock market, the economy, elections, etc. Even though you consciously and mentally know you do not control these sorts of things, because these things affect you, you cannot help but worry and fret over them.

It is here I have to be intellectually honest and admit to a bit of hypocrisy. It's not like I go through life never letting things outside of my control bother me. Everybody, no matter how stoic or indifferent, will still occasionally worry about things outside of their control. We are all human. But at least having the ability to recognize or "catch yourself" when you are unnecessarily fretting over something outside of your control, even occasionally, will still prove beneficial. It will result in less worry and less stress in your life. It will result in better mental health and less depression. And it will allow you to forgive yourself, assuage your guilt, and find peace of mind over a situation you *ultimately are not responsible for*.

It's not easy to develop this mindset, but two quotes I have found help:

"Whatever happens, happens."
        -Spike Spiegel

"Worry is unnecessary interest on a debt that has to be paid."
            -Fortune Cookie that Paraphrased William Inge

While the most obvious and immediate practical application of having this skill would be accepting the election results of 2012, because of the increasing presence of government in our lives the ability to recognize what we do and do not control will prove to have many other uses in the future.

For instance, as the government grows larger and larger, it will crowd out more and more of the private sector. With higher taxation and more government regulation this will result in less economic opportunity for entrepreneurs, innovators, inventors, dreamers and just plain hard workers. Being one of these industrious sorts you may have dreams of starting a company, enriching yourself, or just having a successful career. But with taxation so high, regulations too restrictive, and capital so scarce, your dreams of starting a motorcycle company or inventing a new medical device is nearly impossible. The error you will make (especially men) is blaming yourself for failing to realize your dreams, when in reality it was outside of your control. It was doomed from the beginning. You do yourself no service misplacing the blame on yourself.

Another perfect example (again, disproportionately affecting men) is not being able to provide for your family. Say you work in the construction business circa 2005. The housing market is booming, you're making money, and you can finally afford that trip for you and your family out to Yellowstone. All of the sudden banks start going bankrupt, real estate developers embezzle funds and go overseas, and the whole housing bubble pops. Contracts are cancelled, general contractors aren't paying, and you get laid off.

Why did you get laid off?

The reality is because a bunch of inept bankers, criminal real estate developers, amoral mortgage brokers and corrupt politicians created the world's largest housing bubble. But ironically, the average man during the

Great Recession probably took this personally, illogically blaming his sole self for the *entire financial crisis of 2009*. Worse still, men across America felt an incredible amount of guilt and shame for not being able to provide for their families. And worse than that, how many men committed suicide because of a recession that was not caused by them? All of this can be avoided in mastering the skill of recognizing what you do and do not control.

Now we can go on citing limitless number of examples where it's good to have this skill. But in general the way this skill is going to serve you best is realizing you are in an environment that is becoming progressively more hostile towards the individual. Government spending already accounts for 40% of GDP and given the 2012 election results, it will only get higher. Additionally, there are social consequences to an ever-expanding state as well.

- Would you like a father daughter dance at your local school? Too bad, it's been banned.
- Want to light up a cigarette at a bar? Too bad, it's been banned.
- Want to carry a gun for personal protection? Too bad, it's been banned, besides you're too stupid to be trusted with a gun.
- Want to have a 32 ounce soda in New York City? Too bad, it's been banned, besides you're too stupid to be trusted with your own diet.

These social violations are nothing more than a harbinger of things to come as the government expands and the individual shrinks. Again, all outside of your control.

Ultimately, the key to "learning to let go" is to realize you are just one person in a democracy of 300 million. It isn't the government or the state that you are fighting as much as it is the stupidity of the other 299,999,999 Americans. You by your little lonesome, no matter how right and correct, cannot overcome such odds and will have to suffer the consequences of the majority's ignorance. Acknowledging these lopsided odds allows you to let go and enjoy life. Besides, ignorant people are definitely one of the things you will never control.

There Are Only Fat Chicks in Casper

"The Beacon Club" is the only real dance hall in the town of Casper, Wyoming, and as far as my knowledge tells me, it is the only dance hall in the entire state. Upon moving to Casper I was thankful to have such a dance hall as I enjoy ballroom dancing. However, experience has told me that in order to get the most out of dancing I need a partner who meets some um..."physical qualifications." More bluntly, I'm a smaller fellow and I can't dance with 180 pound heifer of a woman in fear I'd get crushed. Regardless, there I was, my first night heading out to "the Beacon," hopeful to find somebody my size. I was quickly let down when I walked in and realized the average woman in Casper doesn't weigh 180 pounds, but more like 240.

Matters were only made worse due to the demographic make-up of the town. Casper is heavily reliant upon coal, gas and oil meaning there is a disproportionate number of men relative to the number of women. This went a long way in explaining why I would see pretty decent looking guys with absolutely heinous women, and it also explained the cool, if not outright mean reception I'd receive from quite average-looking women when I'd ask them to dance. It wouldn't just be a polite "no thank you," but rather a childish giggle and "whatever" as if I had propositioned them for sex. It wasn't until I went to the senior center that I found an audience of women willing to dance. Of course, dancing with 93 year old Tilly had its drawbacks. You couldn't turn her too fast, you couldn't dip her, and you certainly couldn't flip her. Soon dancing proved so problematic I gave up. It wasn't until I moved out of Casper 8 months later that I had my next dance.

The point I'm trying to make is not one of the fat women in Casper, but one of rational versus realistic expectations.

Was it rational for me to expect there be a HANDFUL of reasonably in shape women capable of dancing in Casper?

Yes.

Was it reasonable of me to expect a certain modicum of courtesy and etiquette when asking them to dance?

Yes.

Was it within the confines of sanity to expect out of a town of 60,000 I should find at least ONE girl who wasn't morbidly obese and would qualify as a dance partner?

Certainly.

But rational as my expectations were, they weren't realistic. There were no such women in Casper. Most of them were overweight. Most of them didn't have the patience or desire to learn to dance. Most of them were not receptive to having an "advance" or request made of them to ballroom dance. And so no matter how reasonable and rational I was being in my expectations, those expectations were trumped by something far more powerful - reality.

Sadly this "rational vs. realistic paradox" applies in another regard when it comes to a pillar of American life. And unfortunately, this pillar is one of our most holy and scared institutions – the American Dream.

The American Dream (typically defined as a house, a career and a family) is not outlandish nor egregious in terms of rational expectations. Most people SHOULD be able to buy a house. Most people SHOULD be able to have a family. Most people SHOULD be able to have a decent career. And most people SHOULD be able to afford children. But with economic growth decreasing and a mandate by the American electorate to pursue socialism the American Dream is not only under threat, but becoming outright impossible for most youth.

First, in order to achieve the American Dream you need money, namely a career. With the Great Recession unemployment has been at European levels and nearly double that for younger generations. This also does not speak to underemployment where some estimates have half of people under 25 working nowhere near their potential. Sure they have a job, but with a master's degree they're only making $9 per hour as the local barista. Further crippling the financial future of most youth is their crushing student debt. Even if they were gainfully employed they still have to service their mountain of student loans, leaving little, if any money for the purchase of a home.

Second, let's talk about the home. Not only have our younger generations suffered an education bubble, they also witnessed the housing bubble. You would think the lower prices that ensued with the popping of the bubble would help them, but unfortunately the consequential government regulation makes it nearly impossible for recent college graduates to qualify for a loan. Worse still are the young go getters who were ahead of the curve and bought property before the bubble burst. Not only are they most likely underwater on their mortgages, they are unlikely to get refinanced because of the sea of red tape they must go through to qualify for HARP, HARP II, HARP III, The Return of HARP and whatever other nonsense has come out of Washington. Finally, the housing bubble and the ensuing financial crisis has put a bad taste in the mouths of any future prospective home buyers. Seeing their parents get foreclosed on, the stress involved with trying to get refinanced, or seeing their friends suffer the same, younger generations view housing as a liability, not an asset. And forever increasing property taxes may prove them right.

Third, most people's American Dream includes a spouse at some point or another. Again, the poor economy and even poorer earnings prospects of young American men make it hard to propose when they can barely afford a wedding ring, let alone their rent. However, what makes this component of the American Dream doubly impossible are the "advances" made by feminism which have simply corrupted the quality and caliber of both men and women, rendering most unmarriageable.

Women, led to believe the lie they can "have it all," are more interested in a Sex in the City lifestyle than marrying and starting a family. Also, with society and government solely focusing on the advancement of women with no regard to men, most American women now suffer from solipsism making them unfit for marriage. Men are no better. With an appalling lack of male role models and male influence in their upbringing they are weak, out of shape, physically unattractive and unmotivated. Spiritually and emotionally they are defeated and indifferent, opting instead to play video games and drink, or worse, they become hipsters, major in the liberal arts and vainly try to live up to the standards feminists have set for them. This results in a dating pool of men who are no longer capable of providing for women who are no longer capable of supporting men, all of which can expect a 50% divorce rate should they be foolish enough to wed.

Fourth and finally, children. Say you were lucky enough to find a qualified spouse. Do you dare risk bringing children into this world? Each one costs an estimated $250,000 – a price tag that is prohibitively expensive. And what about the kids' financial futures themselves? Each child born today is estimated to inherit $200,000 in debt and that says nothing about what kind of economic opportunity (or lack thereof) that child will have in their future. Also, what about the legal risks? False accusations of child abuse, a state all too eager to "educate" and rear your child. And once again, the constantly looming threat of divorce is always a disproportionate threat against men deterring them from starting a family in the first place.

Add all these things up and it's apparent the American Dream is dead. Not only is it too risky in terms of marrying the wrong person and having kids you can't afford, but the economic fundamentals necessary to afford the dream just aren't there. Even if most young Americans wanted to pursue the American Dream they can't simply on the grounds they can't afford it.

Sadly, the demise of the American dream does not end here in that the American Dream went beyond a good-paying job and a nuclear family. It was much more personal. It was what you wanted to do with your life that you enjoyed and made you special. It was what you had a yearning to do, whatever it was, that made you happy. It was what you were going to do with your one finite life on this planet and nobody was going to take it from you. And no matter how great or grandiose that dream, if you tried your best chances are you would succeed, if not have a hell of a time trying.

Only problem is you need a society and an economy conducive to such grandiose ideas. If the economy is only growing at 2% per annum instead of 4%, your lifetime earnings are going to be a fraction of what they normally would be and consequently your dreams must be scaled down. If your taxes keep going up, you have less and less disposable income to pursue your dreams. If regulations keep increasing any commercial dreams you may have are quickly rendered impossible. And if people are raised to be envious of the successful, punishing them with wealth and income confiscation, why work hard in the first place?

So what do we do? Give up on the American Dream? Stay at home, drinking, playing video games?

No.

The psychological adjustment you must make here is one of "making lemonade out of lemons." While yours and mine and everybody else's American Dreams are rapidly being destroyed, that doesn't mean we can't have new ones. Dreams that are not only rational and feasible, but not so fraught with legal and financial risks. However, it is hard to give up on your true American Dreams you fell in love with. How do you decide not to get married? How do you decide not to have kids? How do you accept you will never experience your childhood dreams?

The answer is simple - you have no choice. You must abide by reality.

Returning to our Casper example, no matter how much I wanted to dance, it wasn't going to happen. So what did I do instead? Stay at home? Drink? Play video games?

Well yes, I did those things too, but I also pursued new things that were feasible.

I climbed over 12 peaks in the Big Horn and Rocky Mountain Ranges. I made at least a dozen road trips out west visiting over 15 national parks. I hiked over 300 miles in the most beautiful parts of the country. I attended the Sturgis and Beartooth Path motorcycle rallies. Made a cross country trip to Phoenix and back on my motorcycle. Shot AR-15's every other weekend. Wrote a book. Learned to clean out a carburetor. All of this interspersed with agate hunting, fossil hunting and tornado chasing.

Did I ever get to dance with a reasonably in-shape girl?

No.

Will I ever get to own my own personal P-51 Mustang?

No.

Will I ever get to build my 1960's James Bond Villain Bachelor Pad in the Black Hills and host cocktail parties where Eva Mendes will be in attendance?

Never.

But I did what I *could* and enjoyed every minute of it.

You too must do the same.

Labor vs. Leisure

The final psychological adjustment you must make is living your life in accordance with leisure, not labor. This is not only a large psychological adjustment, but arguably the most difficult one to make because it goes against your biology. Ever since humans have existed it has been hardwired into our genetic programming to work hard. Not because our cave-men ancestors would get promoted to the "Vice President of Rocks" or their hard work would pay off in the form of a Flintstone's Ferrari, but rather for plain and simple survival. In short, if they didn't work hard, they would die. And by default, in working harder they would make their lives more secure. This means your preference for labor is genetically engrained in your DNA.

Second, for Real Americans the desire to work hard is reinforced culturally. You're told if you go to school, study hard, work hard, put the extra time in at the office, you will be successful. The problem here is that it takes at least until you're 30 to realize whether or not this is true. By that time, whether you actually *are* successful or not doesn't matter. It's been engrained in your psychology since kindergarten and you still can't turn it off.

Unfortunately what this means is switching your focus in life from labor to leisure is not as simple as throwing a switch in your brain, making a decision, and then declaring,

"I'm going to opt for leisure instead of working real hard! Where's the beer?! What time is Hogan's Heroes on?!"

It's more difficult than you might think. This is evidenced by a little-known problem that plagues retirees - depression and suicide AFTER retirement.

You might think this is odd – *people getting depressed AFTER they retire???* – but it's actually quite common. Men and women who worked their entire lives, had great careers, and no doubt social networks, find themselves depressed, edgy, and full of angst because for the first time in 50 years they have nothing to do. Also to one extent or another people value and define themselves by what they do for a living. Without that job or career, suddenly they feel like they have no purpose in life and can easily fall into depression or worse.

The problem for us is these people *earned* their retirement. They have every right to retire. They're old, they've put in their dues and yet they *still* suffer from some kind of unwarranted shame or guilt and get depressed. Imagine how hard you're going to have to fight against depression when you aren't even retirement age, you're most likely in your prime, and you still purposely decide to clock out and go Galt.

Since some level of depression is practically guaranteed, we must be able to make this adjustment without becoming depressed. To do this the best way is to ask ourselves why are we choosing leisure over labor in the first place. And it boils down to one simple, but very compelling reason – slavery.

Call it whatever euphemism leftists want – egalitarianism, social justice, progressive taxation, progressivism – it all boils down to that same thing - slavery. One group of people are working and slaving away for another group of people. Yes, people and politicians will try to rationalize it.

"The recipients of welfare are worse off than you."
"The recipients of your tax dollars have been discriminated against/are disadvantaged."
"The woman on EBT is a single mother."

"How dare you not want to help the poor!"

But it still doesn't change the fact that they are economic parasites and you are the host. You are a slave to them.

Normally when I accuse people of parasitism or even discuss it I'm accused of hatred or despisement, but we need to set emotion aside and think literally about this. I am not using the term "parasite" as a pejorative or to irk people, I'm using it as a descriptive noun. That *is what they are*. If you do not support yourself and rely on the production of others you are by *definition* a parasite,

period,

end of discussion,

no two ways about it.

This, by default, makes the people who work and pay the taxes to subsidize these parasites the host or slave. Doesn't matter how the parasites got to the point they needed other people to pay for them. Doesn't matter how noble the parasites' intentions were or how bad their luck was. None of those circumstances changes the fact they are parasites on society. And none of these circumstances change the fact you are their slave.

It is the parasite-host relationship that should give people the anger necessary to forgive themselves for pursuing leisure over labor. It is the word "slave" that should enrage you to the point you can override your genetic hard-wiring and have no regret or depression in opting to "Go Galt." And it is the fact society has confirmed this is the path the country is going to go down that should only reinforce your decision.

Secondly, let's talk about the 2012 election. On its simplest implication, the election has told us the American people wish to tax labor and production more. The election also implies that we will reward leisure more. The incentives of this should be obvious – work less, loaf around more. But what we don't see is the secondary effect this election will have on the economy. An effect that will make it easier for you to decide whether you'd like to work or not. Specifically, a lack of economic growth resulting in a lack of jobs.

In deciding to punish production, people are not only deterred from working, but entrepreneurs, capitalists, industrialists, and all around go-getters are also deterred from creating jobs. So even if you wanted to participate in the labor market, your desire is moot because chances are there won't be any jobs. This lack of jobs essentially makes the decision for you, and the current labor market bears this reality out. The unemployment rate confirms the labor market is still flooded. Underemployment rates show there really are no good jobs out there anyway. And record-high "time spent unemployed" practically proves leisure will be forced upon you. Fighting this economic reality is merely futile.

Finally, if none of this convinces you or somehow doesn't assuage your guilt about early retirement, let's talk about just how much you slave away for other people. The numbers aren't perfect (as not everybody is in the same tax bracket), but as mentioned before, over time government spending has gone from about 5% GDP in the early 1900's to 40% today. This roughly translates into your ***overall tax rate being 40%*** for state, federal, and local taxes.

(the chart below only shows Federal data, not state or local which are roughly an additional 10-15% GDP depending on the state).

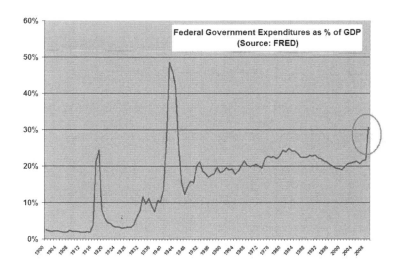

Federal Government Expenditures as % of GDP
(Source: FRED)

However, not all 40% of your money goes to other people. Some of it goes to roads, infrastructure, defense, schools, etc., all of which are considered "public goods" and not income transfers. These budgetary items account for a whopping 30% of the federal budget and roughly the same for state and local budgets. In other words, *70%, SEVENTY PERCENT OF YOUR TAX MONEY GOES TO OTHER PEOPLE*, meaning the government is not an agent of governance as much as it is an agent of wealth-redistribution.

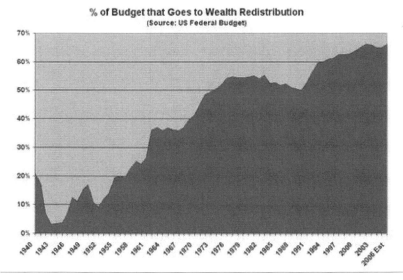

% of Budget that Goes to Wealth Redistribution
(Source: US Federal Budget)

So if 40% of your income goes to a budget where 70% of it is spent on other people, that means *28% OF YOUR TIME IS SPENT BEING A SLAVE OR HOST TO OTHER PARASITES*. More if you're foolish enough to "try hard" and "become successful." Out of a 50 year career that's *14 YEARS OF VACATION* you could have had, but instead you were literally a slave to somebody else for those 14 years.

Drinking scotch and watching Hogan's Heroes at 3PM doesn't sound so bad now, does it?

CHAPTER 2
THE NEW ECONOMIC REALITY

"Where you come from, it's gone.
Where you thought you were going to, weren't never there.
And where you are ain't no good unless you can get away from it."
-Ministry/Jesus Built My Hot Rod

It's one thing to believe, but it's another thing to know. So I find hard
numbers important in that they not only confirm what we suspect, but
also show us mathematically and precisely just how big our problems
really are. Furthermore, numbers eliminate any emotion or feelings
where there shouldn't be any. Normally, this is a problem of the left. The
left loves to "feel" and start off sentences with "well I just feel" or "well I
just think" because they're too damn lazy to get up, turn on the
computer, and look things up so they in fact *know*. However, I fear
because Real Americans love the country so much, we have an emotional
attachment that biases us towards unwarranted optimism about the
future of the United States. Unwarranted optimism that could cause us to
make decisions that are not based in reality and will come to hurt us in
the future.

It is here we must once again exercise the lessons we learned from the
previous chapter and not ask ourselves what we would like to see the
country be or become, but rather what it is and likely to be in the future.
It is only through bravely acknowledging the reality of the situation can
we make fully informed decisions. Fully informed decisions that may be
hard, but will serve us infinitely better than our idealistic ones.

Finally, in understanding the mathematical realities of the economics and
finances of the nation you will be better prepared to make other decisions
that will serve you in other regards. Specifically, decisions about investing,
personal finance, budgeting, strategy, education, where to live, etc., all of
which will help you preserve your wealth and live a better life.

The Decline

First, we must accept that the United States is in decline. It is hard to accept this, but if you don't believe me, let me cite some simple anecdotal evidence comparing what he had in the 1950's versus what we have today:

1950's	Today
Sophia Loren	Madonna and Lady Ga Ga
Cary Grant	Seth Rogen
Shelby Mustang (60's)	Chevy Volt
June Cleaver	Sandra Fluke
Duke Ellington	Snoop Dog
Peter Gunn	"Don't Trust the B in Apartment 23"
Bugs Bunny	Adventure Time
WWII Vets	OWS protesters

I could go on, but no matter which way you slice it, culturally, socially, politically, romantically and economically, the United States is in decline, period. Anybody who is half cognizant of their surroundings knows this.

However, the problem with these various forms of cultural decay is there is no mathematical way to measure it. How do you measure the repulsiveness of Seth Rogen against the suave debonair behavior of Gary Grant? How do you measure the decay from Duke Ellington to "Snoop Dog?" How do you measure the drop in quality from a "June Cleaver" to a Sandra Fluke?

Additionally, much as we Real Americans know these are symptoms of decay, people will counter these are just the tastes and preferences of the people. Tastes and preferences that cannot be judged. Who's to say Sandra Fluke wouldn't make a better wife than June Cleaver? Who's to say Seth Rogen isn't as hot as Cary Grant? Who's to say I can't pick up girls in a Chevy Volt? And who's to say OWS protesters are not of equal or superior moral caliber than WWII vets? These are just evil "paleo-American-patriarchy-centric paradigms" forced upon the innocent masses by bigoted, ignorant right-wingers!

Thankfully the field of economics provides us nearly limitless number of statistics that, though they don't directly speak to or measure specific sociological phenomenon, they do measure the overall health and well-being of the country. Issues that affect everybody regardless of political affiliation and cultural tastes. Furthermore, as it just so happens, the largest problems the US faces are economic. Vomitous as Madonna may be, her popularity is quite irrelevant when debt to GDP is over 100% and people are collecting unemployment for nearly two years. Thus, to get a true read on the current state of our county, our culture, and our economy, our focus will be on economics and we will start with measures of wealth.

Of the literally thousands of economic metrics and statistics, the one that speaks most directly to our economic well-being is the rate of economic growth. The traditional statistic used to gauge this is "GDP" or "Gross Domestic Product" which is defined as:

"All the goods and services produced within a nation's border within one year"

or in even simpler terms

"How big is our economy?"

Obviously, we want GDP growth to be as high as possible. The more our economy grows, the better off we are as a nation. However, this growth must be "real growth" meaning growth absent of inflation. So what economists actually focus on is a slight variant called "real GDP" – GDP that has been adjusted for a change in prices.

When you look at it, "real GDP growth" is naturally very volatile showing no discernible trend one way or another:

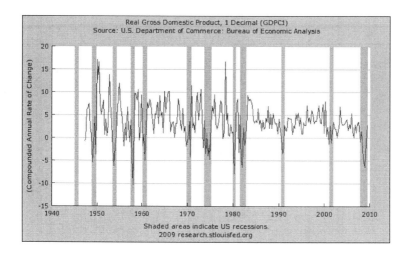

But when we average it out over the course of 20 years we get what I like to call "generational real GDP growth" – i.e. – what is the long term trend of the economic growth of our nation? What we see here is arguably the most telling sign of our decline – our economic growth is slowing. And not just slowing, it is nearly half of what it used to be during our glory days from the 1940's to the 1960's.

During that time our economy was growing at an average of 4.25%. It has since dropped to 2.5%.

To the untrained eye this may not seem all that bad. "What's a mere 2% per year?" one might ask. The problem is in the mathematics of compounding. In losing 2% growth per year, in 50 years you have forfeited economic growth equal to 100% of the original economy. However, the mathematics of compounding are even more powerful than that. Since this is annualized economic growth, that means "growth upon all the growth of previous years" is also forfeited.

Unless you remember exponential functions from your high school algebra class a better way to explain is by translating this into English:

"How big would our economy be if we just kept on growing at the old rate of 4.25%?"

The answer is shocking.

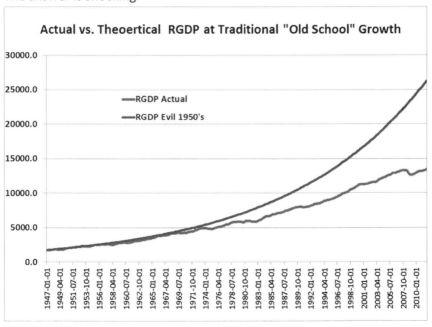

Had the United States economy kept up the average growth rate it had from the 1940's to the 1960's it would be double what it is today. Instead of the current $14 trillion (in 2005 dollars) we have today, we could have had an economy equivalent to $26 trillion.

To make this statistic even more shocking (and personal) what we need to do is adjust it for the number of people living in the country. Economists do this because we are no so much concerned about how much the country is making as a whole, as much as we are what each individual in the country is making. This measure is called "GDP per Capita" which is essentially the same as "Income per Capita"(i.e.-the average amount of money a person can expect to make in a year). Our historical real GDP per capita looks like this:

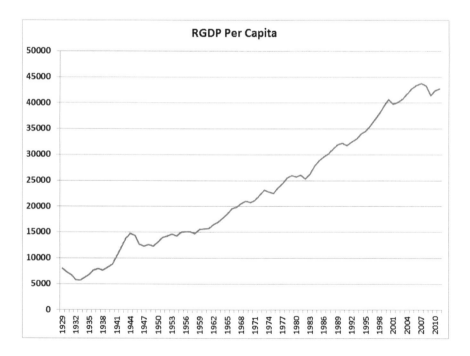

In short the average person in the United States today can expect to make somewhere around $42,000 per year. But had our economy grown at its traditional rate of 4.25% the average person would not be making a paltry $42,000 per year. It would be closer to...

$99,832 (in 2012 dollars)

This means the *average* person in the United States would have been making that coveted "six figure salary" had we just kept doing what we were doing. It's also very likely we'd have nowhere near the financial and debt problems we have today. And imagine what kind of technological advances would have been made had we remained so productive.

"Coulda, shoulda, woulda" all we want, the problem is we didn't. And while we can mourn the loss of what we "could have" accomplished as a country, the true sign of the decline is in our inability to even maintain an INCREASE in our standards of living. Much like "generational real GDP growth" I also calculated the 10-year rolling average in the growth of our "real GDP per capita" to see what is happening to our ability to at least *progress*. Sadly, we're not.

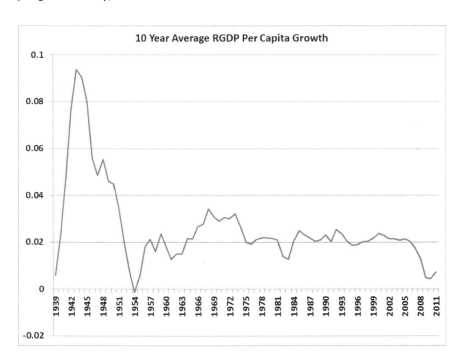

Not since the scaling back of WWII (which caused the dip in 1955 and was also a one-time, non-economically related event) have we had such little increase in our standards of living. Despite the Vietnam War, the oil embargoes of the 70's and the horrible Volcker Recession of the early 80's, the United States STILL managed to provide, on average, an annual improvement of 2% per year in people's standards of living. The past 10 years, however, has essentially delivered 0%. Our standards of living are still below the 2006 peak and until economic growth surpasses population growth, we can expect to remain stagnant as a country, or worse, continue our decline.

Unemployment

As economic growth stagnates and our standards of living decline, it is only a natural consequence employment will suffer too. Of course, it's no secret unemployment is up and people are hurting for jobs, but most people don't realize how serious this current bout of unemployment really is. Furthermore, most people take a superficial look at unemployment, never really pondering the role labor and employment play in their lives, when in reality employment and the labor market play arguably the single largest role in an individual's economic and financial life. The labor market determines what kind of career and what kind of education people should pursue. Subsequently the labor market ultimately determines what kind of a career people *will have*. It will determine what kind of income they earn and thus the standards of living they will enjoy during their entire lives. And it will also have an effect on future generations as the financial well-being of parents does have an effect on their children.

Because of its importance we must look at unemployment and the labor market in two ways. First, what is the current state of the labor market and just how bad is it? And second, what is the labor market telling us before making decisions about what to study, what career to pursue, how much of our finite lives to spend pursuing it...or whether none of it is worthwhile and you'd be better off enjoying the decline? We start with the unemployment rate.

The unemployment rate is the most cited employment statistic in all of economics. It is defined as:

"The percent of the labor force that cannot find a job."

or in English

"The percent of people who want jobs, but can't find any."

Historically, economists consider a 5% unemployment rate "good." You would think "Well, wouldn't 0% be better?" However, 5% is deemed to be the "natural rate" where people willingly quit jobs to pursue better opportunities. Regardless, debates about what is the "natural rate" or what is a "good" unemployment rate are moot because the last time we saw an unemployment rate of 5% was in 2008.

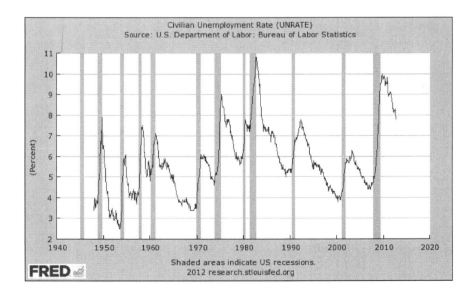

Here there is some debate as to whether or not this economy truly is the "worst economy since the Great Depression." Though not as high during the Volcker Recession in the early 80's, unemployment has remained stubbornly high, failing to drop rapidly after it peaked as is usual for most recessions. Again, these technicalities are moot, not just because of the severity of this particular labor market, but barring some kind of economic miracle this labor market is practically guaranteed to earn the title "worst economy since the Great Depression."

Unfortunately, the employment picture does not improve from here. One of the main reasons is the difference between the "unemployment rate" and the "labor force participation rate." The single biggest misconception about the unemployment rate is that it is the "percent of the POPULATION that can't find jobs." If this were the case, EVERYBODY would be assumed to be looking for jobs. Are you going to have 93 year Gertrude slave away as a barista? Or perhaps force her 6 year old great grandson Tim to slave away in the coal mines? Of course not. Two major groups of people – retirees and children – are obviously not looking for jobs so we don't consider them when we are calculating the unemployment rate; we only consider people officially in the "labor force."

Therefore, a much more important statistic is the "labor force participation rate" or in English, "what percent of able-bodied people are willing to work."

Here we must pay attention to semantics because they have ramifications.

To be considered part of the labor force, you need to be:
1.   Between 16-64
2.   Able to work
3.   and ACTIVELY LOOKING for work

So even if you are an able-bodied 28 year old man with no problems whatsoever, if you decide to go on the government dole and no longer look for a job, you aren't accounted for in the unemployment rate because you are not considered to be part of the labor force.

It is here the "labor force participation rate" is arguably a better measure of the health of our labor market than the unemployment rate because it shows you what percent of the people who can work, actually pursue it.

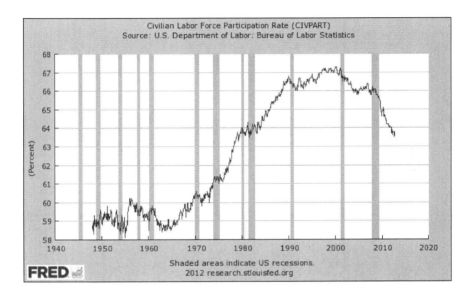

What we see here are two major trends. The first is the dramatic increase in labor force participation primarily due to women entering the work force. The second major trend we see is the severe drop in the labor force participation rate since the beginning of the Great Recession. A full 2% of the population is no longer looking for work, even though they are physically able. This coincides with no demographic or cultural change in the US labor market. It is solely due to people giving up hope and leaving the labor market. In theory this could be added to the current unemployment rate resulting in a "real" unemployment rate closer to 10%.

Sadly, our employment picture only gets worse. Because what is considered "employment?" If you have a doctorate in engineering, but can only work as a stock boy at the local grocer are you really employed? Technically yes, but nowhere near your capacity. This speaks to another problem plaguing this economy - UNDERemployment.

Underemployment is precisely that. You're employed, but nowhere near your capacity. While there are no official figures on underemployment, proxies are used to estimate it, notably the U6 Unemployment Rate.

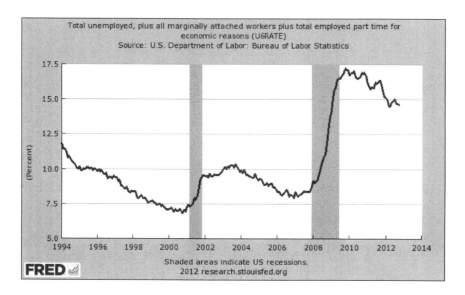

This rate includes those unemployed and those working part-time or deemed "marginally attached" (not fully out of the labor market, but certainly discouraged enough to not give finding a job a full go). This corroborates the limitless number of stories of college graduates who cannot find jobs and are resorting to "any" job just to make ends meet, not to mention pay off their student debts.

The final employment statistic, though not commonly cited, speaks volumes as to the severity of this recession and no doubt clinches the title "Worst Economy Since the Great Depression."

Civilian Unemployment Over 27 Weeks

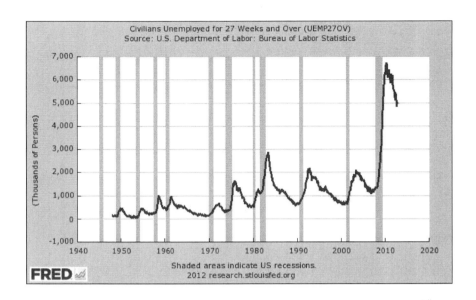

This self-explanatory statistic not only explains why so many people are dropping out of the labor market, but also explains why this recession "feels" worse than others, even though headline statistics (like the unemployment rate) suggest otherwise. Ever since this metric was recorded no recession has even come close to making so much labor lay idle. This even explains the drop in our standards of living and GDP. Having an army of 5 million people laying idle for over 2 years, pro-rated at $42,000 per year, translates into nearly half a trillion dollars of lost GDP.

Now we could go on, as there are many other employment-related statistics, but the larger point is not only to prove just how dire the labor market is, but to show you precisely what the labor market is telling us.

It's saying,

"Don't come here. There are no opportunities here. The path to achieving your dreams and goals do not lie through the US labor market."

The question is whether we are going to listen to what the labor market is saying or ignore it at our own peril. You may think that you're special or you're going to get lucky and land a job despite the unemployment rate. You may think you'll squeak by with your Masters in English and through nepotism land an editor job at a publishing house in New York. Or you may fancy yourself a great networker and be that one All-Star-Ass-Kissing Analyst they hire in the Bulge Bracket.

But you do so at great risk.

For in order to get a job in today's labor market you need to invest an incredible amount of time and resources qualifying yourself. You not only need to get a degree, you need to have the right experience. And not only do you need the right experience, you need to attend the right college. And not only do you need to attend the right college, you need to have the right contacts. And not only do you need to have the right contacts, you need the right certifications. And not only do you need the right certifications, you need the right extra-curricular activities on your resume. The list goes on and on.

By the time it's all said and done, you have spent 4-6 years of your youth pursuing a degree, $100,000 on tuition, another $10,000 on certification programs, and thousands of hours networking, kissing ass, interning and hobnobbing, all to have at best a *marginal* chance of getting hired.

But the real irony is hired for what?

One of those "highly-coveted" jobs in today's corporate America?

One of those smashing careers where your mind is challenged to its greatest limit and you're allowed to achieve your greatest potential?

That's laughable.

The reality is most jobs and careers just plain suck. They never materialize the way they're advertised. They're mundane, they boring, they're life-draining. You're never challenged, you're rarely rewarded, and no matter how smart you are, after years and years of sitting in cubicle after cubicle your mind will atrophy. Jobs are also highly insecure, subject to the whims of the economy, a hostile takeover, a restructuring, or a paranoid, sadistic boss. You suffer office politics, pettiness, and faux harassment complaints, all of which does nothing more than shorten your life expectancy and lessen your standard of living.

In other words, even if you "succeed" in landing a job, you still fail. Most employers are so manipulative and dysfunctional you wouldn't want the job in the first place. Besides, with the labor market so flooded with desperate job-seekers, employers can afford to be arrogant, picky and stingy. This attitude makes most corporate gigs insufferable.

So what's the alternative? Not go to school? Not get some kind of training? Not look for work? Your options, thankfully, are not so black and white.

First, realize there are certain skills and trades that are going to be in demand no matter how bad the economy. Skills and trades we've largely "poo pooed" in the past 40 years: electricians, plumbers, mechanics, welders, etc., Careers English majors love to make fun of, but careers that also make 8 times the amount English majors will ever make. The reason these trades will always be in demand is because even without new economic growth our machines, homes, and equipment will always need service and repair. This is a "worst case" scenario ignoring various economic booms that disproportionately benefit skilled tradesmen (for example the Bakken oil boom has employed many more welders than philosophy majors). Additionally, these trades are "local," meaning they cannot be outsourced to "Punjab" in New Delhi to remotely trouble shoot a computer program over the internet at 50 cents per hour. Finally, the trades have the added benefit of being your own boss. You run your business how you want, make the decisions how you please, and there's no middle management boss being the bane of your existence 8 hours a day. If you are so inclined a career in the trades is a viable and profitable option usually requiring only two years of schooling and no pre-requisite classes in 15th Century Guatemalan Lesbian Poetry.

Second, the United States is not the only country on the planet. It only accounts for 35% of the world's GDP meaning the MAJORITY OF ECONOMIC GROWTH IS OUTSIDE THE US. While it may require you learn a different language, that is a small price to pay to be able to participate in a much healthier labor market in an economy that actually has a future. Will this inconvenience you, forcing you to learn a new culture and a new language?

Yes.

Will this require you adapt a new psychology and leave the comforts and familiarities of home?

Yes.

But if you are to the point like millions of others are (depressed, hopeless, even suicidal) at least entertain the idea of looking overseas for work.

Third, even if you are somewhat apprehensive about picking up and moving the internet has made it incredibly easy to capitalize on a globalizing economy from the comfort of your own home. In short, just because you live in the United States doesn't mean you're relegated to suffer its dying economy. Admittedly, this requires you have a bit of an entrepreneurial spirit and are willing to take clients and conduct business in other countries. It also assumes you are an independent contractor with no employer of your own. However, as the economy worsens and that mythical 1950's job where you work for 35 years and get a gold watch dies, most Americans will inevitably be forced to become independent contractors at one point in their lives or another. Why limit yourself to a dying economy when a simple internet connection opens you up to the world?

Finally, you have one last option – don't work.

Did you already forget the implications of the 2012 election?

Much as it is ingrained in all Real Americans' psyches to work hard and support oneself, it doesn't change the fact the rules have changed. America "spoke" and they want socialism. Are you going to be a fool and work only to be a slave for all the parasites? Or do you accept this new reality and make the logical choices mandated by this new reality?

Here you have two "sub-options" because I know how distasteful the idea of "not working" is to most Real Americans.

One, you can work VERY LITTLE and still get by. If you have no major financial obligations (children, mortgage, etc.) the average person can easily get by on $15,000 per year. This amount can be earned quite easily by either working full time at some menial job, or part time as an independent contractor with some semblance of a skill.

Two, you can just go full parasite opting instead to live off the government. Again, this may be distasteful, but this is the reality forced upon you by the electorate. It's like playing a soccer game and then in the middle of the game the refs change the rules so you can use your hands. However, you decide out of some kind of loyalty or nostalgia to continue to only play with your feet. Good luck winning.

The larger point in regards to employment is that it's not as bad as it may seem. It only requires we make some psychological adaptations and expand our horizons. Most people have been trained to think the 9-5 job for 40 loyal years at the same employer is the way to go, but labor market realities no longer make that a viable option. We have a choice to accept this and base our decisions around this new reality or continue to be delusional about it…

spending 4-8 years getting degrees that will never pay off…

working at jobs that will destroy our minds…

paying taxes that will never benefit us…

wondering on our deathbeds why we wasted such a high percentage of our lives doing so.

Government Spending and Debt

If declining economic growth and dismal employment prospects aren't enough to convince you, arguably the most compelling reason to throw in the towel and enjoy the decline is the size and growth of government. The reason the size of government is so important is because government can only grow at the expense of the individual. Many people erroneously believe that somehow government is this entity unto itself, the size and growth of which has no bearing or effect on the people. When in reality the government can only get its funding and resources by taxing the production of its own people. So if the government wants to offer free kittens to every child in America, it has to get that money from somewhere, and the only way it can do this is by taxing its citizens. In short the relationship between the government and its people is parasitic - any increase in the size of government has to be paid for by its people, thereby necessarily lessening the individual.

The single best way to measure how much of a role the government plays in the US economy is a simple metric – government spending as a percent of GDP. Since GDP is the size of our economy, taking the budgets of all levels of government (state, federal and local) and dividing it by GDP shows us essentially what percent of the economy is government.

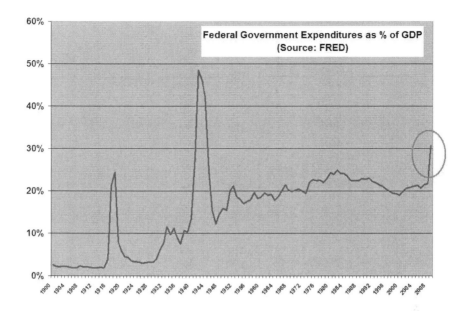

Federal Government Expenditures as % of GDP
(Source: FRED)

Barring instances of world war, we see the general trend has been for government to grow. Federal spending has gone from 3% GDP in the early 1900's to over 30% today (imagine having a tax rate of only 3%!). And this says nothing about state and local spending, which can easily add another 10-15% depending on the state you live in. In short this roughly correlates to a tax rate of around 40%, sometimes easily over 50% depending on your state.

While leftists will claim it's spurious, knowing the government can only grow at the expense of its people, it should be no surprise then that as the government has grown our economic growth has slowed. When we juxtapose the "Generational Real GDP Growth Rate" discussed previously against government's size as a percent of GDP, it shows us just how clear and strong this relationship is.

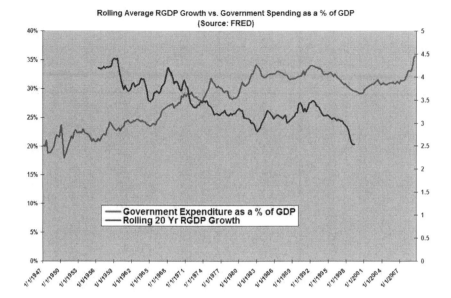

Rolling Average RGDP Growth vs. Government Spending as a % of GDP
(Source: FRED)

The problem is this logical and empirically-proven relationship is lost on the spectacularly ignorant electorate of the United States. Too lazy to ponder the relationship between the state and the people, let alone the risks of an ever-growing state, in 2012 the American people jettisoned their stewardship of democracy and decided to double down on the strategy of expanding the state. This will only prove to worsen our economic problems, not solve them.

Looking at spending as a percent of GDP only focuses on one side of the equation – *spending*. It says nothing about how much money the government actually takes in via taxes, i.e.- *revenue*. Here you can do the same mathematical calculation and convert government revenue as a percent of GDP.

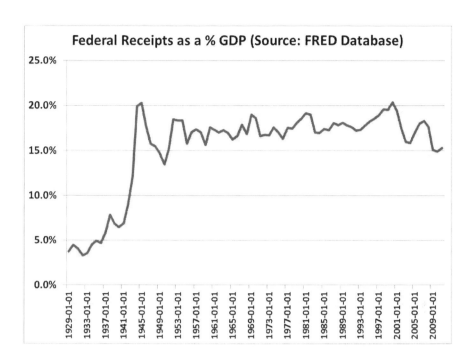

Critics (namely Keynesians) will claim this is the true tax rate a country faces and not spending as a percent of GDP because it does after all show *revenue* as a percent of GDP. However, this is not a matter of professional opinion among economists; it's a matter of them being patently wrong and poor economists. The reason why is regardless of how much money the government brings in through revenues, if it spends more you get a deficit. Over time these deficits accumulate into a "debt" which can only be paid back with...

additional future taxation.

In other words spending more than government takes in merely postpones or defers those taxes into the future. It doesn't eliminate those taxes and if anything, it increases the overall tax burden due to compounding interest on an ever-growing debt.

Jaw-dropping incompetence of Keynesians economists aside, this brings up another important issue – deficit spending. With government spending regularly exceeding government revenues, the United States has historically run deficits. These deficits can also be converted to a percent of GDP to measure just how large and severe these deficits are.

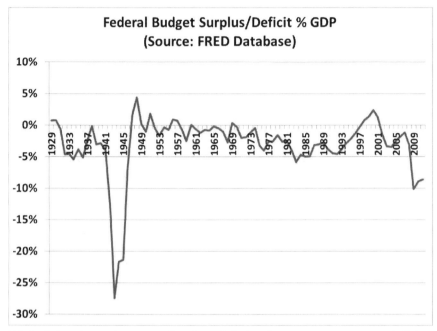

While it has been the norm for the US federal government to run deficits, the deficits run during WWII stand out as exceptionally large. However, this makes sense because when a country's very own existence is threatened, a country will exhaust whatever options it has to in order to ensure its survival. But of larger concern is the deficit spending during times of peace, notably the jump in deficit spending under the Obama administration.

Theoretically at least, you would think the government would run a balanced budget during peacetime or (dare I suggest) a SURPLUS to create a "rainy day fund." Unfortunately, as shown before, the government has become an agent of wealth redistribution, not governance. This means politicians have great incentive to spend money on various social programs, effectively bribing people into voting for them. But the particularly cunning aspect of this plan is the use of debt to postpone the payment of those services. In borrowing the money to pay for these services the people get to enjoy the benefits of government spending without the commensurate increase in taxes to pay for them. If the plan is pulled off perfectly, not only the people, but the politicians die before the debt is called due forcing future "sucker" generations to pay for the previous generation's spending binge. In short, they may not cheat death, but they did cheat taxes.

Inevitably such financial sins build up and just like "deficits as a percentage of GDP" we can also measure "debt to GDP." Debt is nothing more than the accumulated deficits the government has run in the past. Just like if you spent $4,000 more than you took in for three years, your "deficit" would be $4,000 per year, while your total debt at the end of those three years would be $12,000. The federal debt however is just a tad bit larger - $16 trillion.

When it gets to numbers like "trillions" and "billions" the numbers are so large people start to lose the ability comprehend and conceive just what these numbers represent. So again we convert them to GDP to provide a ratio that is more digestible and understandable. When we do the picture is not pretty.

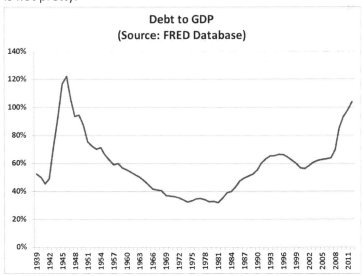

To be blunt the federal debt is the largest it has ever been barring times of war. With no major external threat (such as a war) there is no reason for government spending and consequently debt, to be so high. At $16 trillion the gross federal debt is over 100% the size of our economy, meaning if everybody worked for a year and ALL of our money was taxed, leaving no money for food, clothing or shelter, it still wouldn't be enough to pay off our debt. Each man, woman and child would have to pay $53,000 each to retire the national debt and that once again assumes Gertrude is working as a barista and little Timmy is working the coal mines.

The implications of this debt, combined with the fact 70% of the federal budget is spent on wealth redistribution, sadly only confirms the worst of our fears. Previous generations, ignorant about basic public financing, didn't bother to think about the financial consequences of profligate government spending. Believing things like "poverty," "drugs" and "education" simply required more government money (instead of temerity, rigor, and hard work on the part of the people) our stewards merely indebted the nation, enslaved their own children, all with the added benefit of solving none of those social problems. The people responsible for this financial train wreck will die before paying the consequences, leaving the bill instead to innocent future generations...or at least those naïve enough to keep slaving away and paying taxes.

Promises, Promises

If you'd like a silver lining or some sliver of hope, unfortunately there is none. It only gets worse from here. Because all the debt that has been accumulated in the past is precisely that – debt accumulated in the past. It says nothing about the debt we're going to accumulate in the future, primarily by paying for the future entitlement obligations we promised ourselves.

The amount of stuff we've promised ourselves through the government is literally unlimited. Social security, Medicare, Medicaid, welfare, unemployment, the list goes on and on. And while 104% debt to GDP is bad today, that is nothing compared to what is about to hit us. Estimates vary widely, but just social security, Medicare and Medicaid alone are estimated to be underfunded by $45 trillion. This means we will either have to raise taxes by $45 trillion or borrow an additional $45 trillion to pay for these programs. You add that $45 trillion to the already existing $16 trillion in federal debt and you have total debt obligations equivalent to 400% GDP. This means anybody born today is already on the hook for $200,000 in debt they had nothing to do with.

The question is whether or not the US has the economic productive capacity to make good on all these promises and the answer is, quite frankly, "no." Simplifying the math (a lot) the $60 trillion shortfall we have over the next 75 years implies we need an additional $800 billion in economic growth each year (all of which would be taxed with the unrealistic assumption this would not have an effect on future economic growth). That implies GDP growth would have to be TRIPLE of what it is today. Of course this does not factor in the power of compounding, but even if we did (not to belabor the math lesson), the economy would need to grow at a very rough average of 3% per year, not the 2.25% we're averaging now. This also makes the incredibly optimistic assumption we balance the budget tomorrow and keep it that way for the next 75 years. Not only does the current administration lack the financial fortitude to do that, the average American lacks the work ethic and innovation to deliver the required economic growth. This leads us to arguably the darkest aspect of the government's finances – confiscation.

Unless entitlements are cut, the $60 trillion is going to have to come from somewhere. Tax revenue is an unlikely source in that the government has grown so big already; any further increase will likely crowd out the private sector resulting in lower economic growth and therefore less tax revenues. Borrowing is also an unlikely source because inevitably our creditors (namely the Chinese, Arabs and other US debt holders) will cut us off realizing we have no ability to pay it back. This leaves the federal government with three remaining options:

1. Inflate their way out of this current mess
2. Repudiate the debt (meaning refuse to pay it and default)
3. Tax or confiscate wealth

While inflation is certainly a possibility, printing off $60 trillion in new money would trigger hyperinflation akin to the Weimar Republic. Economic growth would tank, the dollar would collapse, and nobody would loan us any more money after we purposely and knowingly devalued our currency. However, even Obama's economists know you "just can't print off more money" and so this is an unlikely option (though some will contest this is already happening with various Federal Reserve actions such as QE- "X").

Repudiating the debt would be effectively the same thing. Whether we print off trillions of worthless pieces of paper with a lot of zeros on them and use that worthless currency to pay off our debts, or we simply refuse to pay, the effect is the same: We destroy the value of the dollar, we stiff our creditors, and we irreparably damage our economy. The Chinese Imperial Fleet will pay San Francisco Bay a visit just the same, and so this is an unlikely outcome as well.

What is more likely is a "wealth" tax or the outright confiscation of wealth.

Here we need to discern between income and wealth as many people do not know the difference. Income is what you make. Your annual salary, your weekly wage. That is taxed at the various income tax rates at the state and federal levels. A wealth tax is a tax on something you already bought and paid for, something you own. For example you pay property taxes on your home. You didn't have to make income that year to pay the tax. You pay regardless of whether you have income or not simply because you have "wealth," you have a home.

Normally when we think of a wealth tax we think of property taxes, estate taxes or car registration fees. But there is a nice conglomeration of wealth nobody has dared to think would be taxable. And not just taxable, but easily stolen as well.

Your retirement plans.

Estimates vary, but there is roughly $18 trillion invested in the various IRA, 401k and 403b retirement plans. This also says nothing about the trillions more invested in regular ole brokerage accounts earmarked for retirement. Even though it doesn't come close to closing the $60 trillion gap, such a large and liquid pot of gold is irresistible to our progressively socialist politicians looking for perpetual re-election. Here we enter "conspiracy theory territory" where only "crazy right-wingers" imply such things as scare tactics to discredit the lovable and well-intending socialists. The only problem is it's happened before and quite recently as well.

In 2008 Argentina stole the private pensions of its workers, nationalizing those funds to deal with their own debt problems. Bolivia did the same in 2010, as did Hungary. And Bulgaria did their own scaled-down version of confiscating people's private pensions in 2011. Of course, those are just no-name South American countries and backwater Eastern European countries. That can't happen here in America! Why, we're Americans! We have rights!

Unfortunately, the Democrats took note of what Argentina did in 2008 and have since bantered around ideas of rescinding the tax benefits of those programs, even outright nationalizing them. There was hope with the Republican backlash of 2010 that such outright theft would be made impossible, but with the 2012 election decidedly going left, socialist politicians' chops have been re-whetted for a piece of your IRA pie. Ultimately, however, the real risk is not so much the political desires of socialist politicians, but that the economic situation is so dire it will essentially force the decision to confiscate people's retirement accounts. That is the true risk of promising ourselves everything.

Your New Economic Reality

Whether we'd like to admit it or not, the fact remains the US economy, in its current state, is not sustainable or feasible in the long run. It will collapse. Any chance of turning it around and having a viable economic future was destroyed when the American people voted for hope and change instead of reality and math. This once again forces us to deal with "what is" and not "what we'd like things to be." But what is enraging about this particular situation is not so much being forced to accept a reality we don't like, but something far worse - we are no longer in control our own economic success or future. That is becoming the role of the state.

Many people will contest this is too dire, pointing out the US is not a dictatorship wherein some tyrant or another is barking orders telling you what to do. You get to choose what you pursue as a career, buy what you want, and live where you want. However, what people fail to realize is just how intrusive and invasive government has already become in their lives. With the government growing from nearly nothing to nearly half the economy, it has become so large, so pervasive, that it is nearly impossible to do anything without it. Sure you can start a plumbing business, but nearly 40% of your profits will be confiscated making the government a de facto 40% shareholder. Sure you can work hard and have a successful career, but the government will take a progressively larger share of your earnings, making you a slave for a progressively higher percentage of your life. Sure you can own property...well...you don't really "own it" because in paying property taxes you're really renting it from the county, but we'll let you believe you own it. With government spending accounting for 40% of GDP it is just plain inescapable that it will demand an equivalent percentage of your life.

Furthermore, fine, while the government doesn't explicitly deny you the right or opportunity to pursue any particular venture, it does so by default in crowding out the private sector. You can have all the dreams in the world about starting a new motorcycle company, inventing a new fuel, or becoming the world's greatest dachshund herder. But if the government consumes 70% of GDP to pay for old, infirm, or unproductive people simply just to live, there is no capital left to start a business, let alone disposable income to buy your goods. The economic environment has become so poor it makes it impossible for most people to chase their dreams.

But by far the worst consequence of the government growing at the expense of the individual is the dependency the government force-places on its people. With government consuming 40% of GDP it's almost impossible to live life without collecting some form of a government check or subsidy. And when it comes time to make good on all these entitlement programs, estimates have the government consuming closer to 60% GDP, making true independence nearly impossible. The price that will be paid is not going to be the shame or guilt in collecting a government check; instead it will be the death of the individual. Once an individual realizes his or her dreams are no longer feasible and they need the state to live, they will cease being individuals and instead become part of the state commune or "Borg." They will have no future.

In short, the US government has gone from a minimalist-governing entity that served the people by leaving them be and letting them be productive as possible, to a tool of the parasitic classes to confiscate the wealth of the productive classes. And while no society is without its parasites, so numerous and so voracious is the parasitic class in the United States it's on the precipice of killing its host. The only reason the host hasn't complete up and keeled over is because the political class has managed to post-pone the true price of the country's social spending orgy into the future. But that price will inevitably have to be paid.

This puts any member of the productive class or Real Americans in a real quandary.

You can't study hard and work hard because you'll only end up being a slave to the state.

You can't scrimp, budget and save so that someday you can invest in a house or an asset, because the state will merely take it away.

You can't pursue your dreams, starting a company or creating a new invention, because the economy is so poor and government regulation so burdensome, they won't allow for it.

And you dare don't be an individual and aim for success, because the parasitic classes will envy you and use the state to steal your success.

So how do you enjoy the decline in such an economic environment?

You learn the "Art of Minimalism."

CHAPTER 3
THE ART OF MINIMALISM

"Work is a necessary evil to be avoided."
-Mark Twain

In the ideal world the relationship between the state and its people would be "symbiotic." Though this term is normally used to describe relationships between different types of animals, "symbiotic" essentially means "mutually beneficial." For example the seemingly lazy birds sitting atop large African animals such as hippos or elephants are not freeloaders too lazy to fly. They are eating parasites such as fleas and ticks off the larger animals. The bird gets a free meal, the hippo gets rid of his ticks, both parties win. Ideally the same principle would apply to government-citizen relations. The state provides the people with roads, infrastructure, a fair legal system, defense and other things necessary for economic growth, while the people in return provide the economic production and thus the tax base required to finance the state. The state serves the people, the people excel and thrive, and a great society is born.

While this may have been the case at the founding of the country, unfortunately the relationship between the state and its citizenry has become parasitic. This fact is no better highlighted than in the previously mentioned chart showing a full 70% of government spending going to income transfers. These income transfers are parasitic in nature in that they benefit a *specific group of people* instead of investments, infrastructure, roads, defense, and other public goods which benefits *everyone*. Sadly, this relationship is becoming even more parasitic as per the wishes of the American electorate.

The problem in changing the relationship a state has with its people is that it essentially rewrites the entire rules for the game of life. What was sage advice before, no longer applies to the future. What was a guarantee in the past, is certainly not a guarantee now. And while you may have had faith in your institutions, you now fear and distrust them. The question is how do you as an individual adapt or change your behavior when your relationship with the state changes from a symbiotic one to that of a parasitical one?

The answers, unsurprisingly, are identical to that of parasitical relationships in the animal kingdom.

One option is to kill the parasite. Translated literally this would mean "kill" the government, replacing it with a government that would reinstitute a symbiotic relation with its people. The problem is since this is a democracy you would have to "kill the people" who put the government in power. Doing so would not only be a violation of democracy (and our principles) it would result in genocide on par with Stalin, Mao Tse Tung and other heroes of the left.

A second option is to simply leave. You remove yourself from the parasite denying it the opportunity to continue living off of you. In the real world this would be akin something like capital flight or investing overseas. Not everybody has that option, but it is an option that will be discussed in a later chapter.

The third option is to minimize the host in an effort to starve out the parasite. This would mean minimizing yourself, scaling yourself down so the government has less and less resources to steal.

This third option is called "minimalism" and is the optimal of the three.

Minimalism

While I'm a big advocate of capital flight and voting with your feet, the truth is most people are too rooted and attached emotionally, psychologically, socially, and professionally to their current location. When push comes to shove family, friends and loved ones outrank money and are the primary reasons most people, no matter what they say, simply will not leave the United States. Therefore, the option most likely to be availed by most Americans is minimalism. However, this doesn't mean pursuing a strategy of minimalism mutually excludes capital flight as an option. You always will have the option to leave, and even if you don't leave, you have the ability to invest overseas. It's just that minimalism is a more conducive and realistic strategy considering people's emotional attachment to loved ones and home. But what precisely is "minimalism" and what does pursuing it mean for the average person?

While there is no official definition, minimalism is essentially shrinking your economic production to its absolute minimum. There are many reasons to do this, but the primary one is to lessen the amount of wealth or income a parasitical state (or people) can take.

At the core of the "minimalism philosophy" is the element of time. Most people think pursuing a minimalism strategy is so you don't have to pay as much money to the government, when in reality it is more about freedom. Understand you are mortal. You have a finite life. You will die and when all is said and done it doesn't matter how much money you made. The sole single resource you got to enjoy on this planet was your time. When the relationship between the state and the people is symbiotic, then it pays to convert some of this precious time into money through labor. But as a state becomes more and more parasitic, it pays less and less to sacrifice your precious time. The great thing, however, about time is it is not tangible. Only unless you convert it into money through labor does it become tangible and thus taxable and confiscatable. And since the government (unless tyrannical) cannot force you to work, in choosing not to work you make it impossible for the government to steal your time, and thus your life.

Ultimately, this revisits the labor versus leisure decision you have to make. Is it worth slaving away70 hours a week for $100,000 a year gross, but take home of only $45,000? Or is it better to loaf around for 20 hours a week, making only $30,000 a year gross, but $25,000 net? While this decision is of course a personal one, it also hinges on another important aspect of minimalism:

Just how little you can get by on.

Here is where minimalism goes from a tactic to an art or even a lifestyle.

In my great western adventures I was fortunate enough to meet many readers, one of which was "The Great Sage of Utah." The Great Sage read I was coming to town and was kind enough to invite me over for breakfast. Up until meeting him I had prided myself on my ability to get by on very little. In the 90's I was able to pay for college, in full, including living expenses all on about $15,000 per year. In my twenties I lived in a renovated basement so I could rent out an additional unit in a duplex that I owned. And it wasn't until very recently that I decided to stop sleeping at waysides in my car while on road trips. I am an incredibly cheap guy.

But The Great Sage of Utah did me one better.

Renting a small one bedroom, he lived by himself. He didn't go out much, didn't have a car, and relied on public transportation by choice. His furniture consisted of hand me downs, the only real new equipment being his entertainment system. And any food or supplies he had were of the generic knock-off brand variety. But where he really beat me was when he broke the "Holy and Sacred Code of Bachelors" and decided to ….

COOK BREAKFAST AT HOME!!!

It was here I knew I was outdone. There was no way I could compete with that.

So out of curiosity I asked him how much he needed to live and I was not surprised when he said, "About $11,000 per year." This jived with my numbers in that I came in around $13,000, willing to splurge on outsourcing my food preparation.

Most Americans today cannot fathom living on only $11,000 per year. Not only do they make on average around $42,000 per year, they usually spend more than that racking up credit card debts and third mortgages on their homes. The question then is what kind of lifestyle can a person lead with so little money?

Here it depends on the individual and just how "extreme" you care to go. The average person who is purposely minimizing their lives can comfortably get by on around $15,000/year. This certainly isn't a luxurious lifestyle, but it isn't a "no frills" existence either. This includes going out occasionally, taking a vacation or two a year, having an evening cocktail at your favorite bar and paying all your bills. It also assumes, however, this is for one adult person, living in a studio apartment or a rented room, living close to work (if commuting at all) and driving a cheap used car. It also assumes you're not blowing all your money on clothes or shoes, drinking $8 coffee every morning, eating sushi every night, and getting your Master's in Music Therapy. It takes some discipline and self-control, but I know this is all possible because I've been doing it for the past six years.

Basic Tenets of Minimalism

Naturally the above will not work for everybody in that there is no one size fits all program. Some people have kids, others have health conditions, etc. etc. However, there are some basic universal rules or tenets of minimalism that will benefit everyone regardless of their individual situation.

Housing – Housing is the single most important item in a minimalistic lifestyle in that it tends to be your single largest expense. If you can minimize what you're paying each month for housing then you're already halfway there. In general I recommend renting over buying in most circumstances because it grants you freedom and mobility, as well as frees you from the liability of property taxes. But if you have a family and a stable job, then a house could be the way to go. You don't want to live in squalor, but you certainly don't want any more housing than you need. The primary principle that should govern your decision about housing is:

"Where is the cheapest, smallest, optimally located place I can sleep that has just enough room to store me and my stuff?"

More often than not this means renting a studio, a small one bedroom, or a room from a buddy.

Get Rid of Your Stuff – Directly related to housing is stuff. Namely, getting rid of it.

Most people don't realize this, but you pay for stuff thrice. First when you buy it. Second when you store it. And third when you move it. A lot of people will say, "But I don't store my stuff! It's in my apartment!" The problem is you are storing it – *in your apartment.* Stuff takes up space. That means you need more square footage when looking for housing, which means you get to pay more in rent. You also get to pay more in moving expenses since more stuff means you need a bigger, more expensive truck. And none of this speaks to the true cost incurred when moving your stuff - the physical torture involved in actually moving it.

You may be laughing now, but on a more serious note people woefully underappreciate what getting rid of your stuff can do for your finances. Though it may be extreme, consider the benefits if you achieved what a minimalist "purist" would contend is ideal – being able to fit all your worldly possessions in a backpack.

First, your housing requirements would be nothing. Theoretically, you could live in your car (and there are actually communities that do on purpose). But right off the bat your rent could be as low at $200 a month sleeping in a buddy's basement. Most people's financial problems would disappear overnight if they only had to pay $200 a month in rent.

Second, the freedom you'd have would be limitless. You could go anywhere, anytime, with no consequence. You have everything you need in that backpack. In having no home, the world is your home. Go to Mexico, go to Glacier National Park, go wherever you want. No physical thing is holding you back.

Third, maintenance. What house do you have to repair? What furniture do you need to replace? What suits need dry cleaning? What pet needs to be fed? Without stuff, there is no expense maintaining them.

Finally, it's not like you would go without stuff. The kind men and women at companies like Wal-Mart, Target, and Amazon are only more than happy to pay for the rent, heat, electric and overhead to store your stuff for free! It's just a matter of you going there and getting it at your convenience.

Now of course I'm not suggesting anybody live this sort of life, but I am using it to open your eyes as to just how expensive stuff is. If you can get rid of most of your stuff and let the kind people of Wal-Mart and Target store it until you need it, you will have made a great stride in achieving minimalism.

No Children – While I'm not saying "don't have children," children are *very expensive* "stuffs." The average kid costs $250,000 to raise and that doesn't even include college tuition. Also, unlike your X-Box or your computer, they bring in communicable diseases. I have also found out they do not have "off buttons" and the authorities frown on it if you try to sell them. If you already have children or you really want children, by all means certainly have them. But if you can do without, it certainly makes Going Galt a lot easier.

Buy Used – Second to housing and college, your largest purchases are going to be big ticket items. Things like cars, electronics, appliances, etc.

There's no reason to get them new. Besides, unless the economy improves you can expect a never-ending and heavily discounted supply of these items on Craigslist or at your local pawn shop.

Repair and Fix Things – In buying used instead of new, learning to repair and fix things becomes another vital component of minimalism. Being a good mechanic, a good carpenter, or an all-around handyman has many benefits. First, if you are pursuing minimalism then you should have a fair amount of spare time for maintenance and repair. Second, even if you have no experience as a handyman, YouTube has a do-it-yourself video for pretty much every type of household or automotive repair you'll ever need. Third, you'll become more proficient at repairing things, not only cutting down on the time it takes to repair things, but improving your skills along the way to the point where you could barter. Fourth, you'll save a lot of money. Fifth, money that was never transacted and therefore not taxable. And finally, chicks dig guys when they get all greasy and dirty working on cars and motorcycles. One of the best investments you can make as a minimalist is to buy a good set of tools.

Coupons and Deals – One thing I will never understand about feminism is who originally villainized what was traditionally considered "women's work?" The reason I ask is because "women's work" was no less valuable than "men's work." Oh sure, the focus was on what the man did for a living, what was his salary, and how much he made. But nobody ever looked at the other side of the coin and asked how much was spent. It is here that (traditionally) women played a vital economic role in the finances of the family, namely increasing purchasing power.

By becoming experts at finding deals, clipping coupons, and comparing prices women made sure the money the men made went the furthest. Maybe it wasn't as glorious as going to a downtown office and working on some project, but it was just as important and remains so today for your average minimalist.

Since you will be making as little as possible, the art of frugality and stretching a dollar is vital to your budgeting. This isn't to say you go and clip coupons (though it doesn't hurt), but you do wait for things to go on sale. You go to the thrift store or Goodwill. You wait for happy hour, or you just drink at home. You take the extra effort to ensure you derive the most purchasing power from your limited dollars. The alternative is working harder, paying more in taxes, suffering a boss and not enjoying the decline.

Do Not Save for Retirement – While I will explain in more detail in a later chapter, it is advisable you do NOT save for retirement. This sounds counterintuitive, but (given the risk of confiscation previously discussed) contributing to a retirement program is the OPPOSITE of minimalizing yourself. You are unnecessarily exposing yourself and converting your time into a tangible asset that can be confiscated in the future. Thankfully not contributing to a retirement plan frees up a couple hundred dollars a month for you to go and enjoy the decline. The trick is to let go of the guilt many people will have in not saving for retirement.

Start Your Own Side Business – If you only need $15,000 a year to live, why not earn it doing something you enjoy? Yes, you could work for an employer, but most jobs that are going to pay $15,000 a year or let you work part time as such are likely to be menial and unrewarding. Besides, there are some fringe benefits to having your own company. You get to write things off you normally wouldn't (lowering what little you pay in taxes even more). You can always scale your work to the amount of money you need. And there's always the priceless and non-taxable benefit of having no boss to answer to. Keep in mind most businesses do take some time to develop, so it's unlikely you'll be making $15,000 the first year in business. But with the amount of free time minimalism affords you why not make your passion your career?

Catastrophic Health Insurance – Most people complain about the cost of health insurance. Well…"most people" meaning people who *have to have* *the absolute best most comprehensive coverage.* The people who when little Jimmy coughs they rush him to the emergency room. People who insurance companies know are sue-happy and price the premiums accordingly. Those are considered "comprehensive health insurance" plans. For a minimalist, you only need one type of health insurance – catastrophic health insurance.

"Catastrophic" health insurance will not pay for Jimmy's little bandaid or even little Suzie's cast, but it will pay for a heart attack, a car crash or something that actually threatens your life and your finances. In short, it's only for genuine emergencies. And since you're not some soccer mom, rushing your kid to the hospital every time he sneezes the costs are much cheaper. All you do in paying for a "comprehensive" health insurance plan is subsidize those that consume the most health services:

1. Children
2. Women
3. Old people

Be smart, get a plan that benefits you and only you. Costs vary state to state, but you should be able to find something below $150/month as opposed to a comprehensive plan which can easily run $500/month.

Go to School for Trades, Not "An Education" – If you only need $15,000 per year, what is the point in going to college? You can just work any ole job, bank the money, and save four years of your life and $50,000 in tuition. However, there is some merit in getting at least *some* education, specifically a trade.

A trade, unlike a degree, is scalable. A plumber can determine how many contracts he wants to work. A computer networker can determine how many routers he wants to set up. And a chimney sweeper can determine how many chimneys he cleans. But if you get a degree most of the jobs available to you are going to be salaried, meaning you have to put in 40+

hours per week. You can't just work 10 hours per week or four months of the year and quit, saying,

"Well, I made my $15,000! I'll see you in eight months!"

The other major reason you want to get some kind skill or trade is because it increases the amount of free time you will have. I envy one of my friends who is a high-end computer networker. He charges $200 per hour. He only has to work two hours per week, and chooses to, simply because he lives such a Spartan lifestyle. You too can be in this enviable position...or you can work full time as a stock boy for $7.50 an hour.

Elope, No Weddings – Ladies if you really love the man you will be honest enough to admit that "your day" has everything to do with you and nobody else. A very expensive, fleeting, temporary day that will cripple your finances for the next 7 years which in turn will increase your chances for divorce, thus negating "your day." Elope instead. The average wedding costs around $20,000. That's enough to last a minimalist couple a year travelling around the world.

Entertain at Home – If I want to see a movie, I have two choices. Drive, wait in line, drop $12 a ticket, suffer some pathetic-excuse-of-a-parent's children crying, while trying to sneak a beer into the theater,

or

I can just stay at home, Redbox or Netflix the movie, watch it in stunning quality on my LCD projector, with surround sound, all while nursing a scotch served to me by my long-legged girlfriend.

While it may cost a bit, it is wise to make an investment in entertainment equipment at home. Not just electronics, but any entertainment (booze, bar, games, etc.). The reason why is you'll save money, time, and gas by not going out. This doesn't mean you become a hermit, but by staying in for your entertainment and hosting friends at home you will easily recoup the investment you made in a few short years.

Get a Motorcycle – Though optional a motorcycle actually does help achieve an element of minimalism in that it is cheap transportation. You get great gas mileage, maintenance and repair is quite easy, they're fun as hell, plus chicks dig motorcycles. I also believe for a minimalist a motorcycle is the quintessential statement piece. Nothing says, "independent maverick doing their own thing, living their own life" than a bike. Complete the minimalism motif. Get yourself a motorcycle.

Now there are many things more you can nip and tuck to create a minimalist lifestyle, but in the end you will develop your own personal minimalist strategy tailored to your life. Additionally, you will develop a psychology that makes the minimalist life second nature. You may go through withdrawal at first, scaling down from a three bedroom, two bathroom house to just a studio apartment, and you may miss all those beer cars you kept from college, but in the end as the money rolls in and you sleep in till noon, you'll find it to be a much more enjoyable life.

***

Benefits of Minimalism

While lower taxes and a shorter work week are the obvious benefits of minimalism there are other benefits not realized until you're actually practicing it. Benefits that are not only unexpected, but much larger than you would have thought. And while it may seem a risky proposition to give up that reliable 9-5 job, these benefits are so compelling, they actually make the 9-5 job the riskier choice.

Freedom from Employers –The value of having no boss, or making so little you needn't be subjected to the psychotic whims of a boss, is probably the single largest benefit to minimalism. Having the ability to just walk off the job if being treated unfairly is worth at least $50,000 in non-taxable income. There are also health and psychological benefits in not having to deal with abusive and dishonest employers. Lower blood pressure, less stress, lower risk of stroke, all because you had the fiscal discipline to make it so your boss is not necessary for your life. This benefit will only increase in value as it is my sincere belief a flooded labor market, with increasingly desperate people, has put most employers on a power trip. They are becoming more controlling, demanding, sadistic, and dishonest to the point I don't believe anybody can work for one employer for 10 years and not suffer some kind of psychological damage. Employment is a losing proposition. Minimalism gives you the option not to take it.

Better Mental and Physical Health – Directly related to working less is improved mental health. With more leisure and less financial demands the amount of stress you will suffer is a fraction of what most of your full-time counterparts will. Additionally, you can sleep in, eat healthier and exercise more improving your physical health and increasing your life expectancy.

A Better Social Life – In having more leisure naturally you will have an improved social life. Coffee in the morning, cigars in the afternoon, cocktails in the evening, whatever you want to do with your Mondays. You can join clubs, take classes, learn to dance, all those things you wanted to do but "couldn't" because you had to work. Along the way it is a guarantee you are going to meet new people and develop new friendships, making your life even more rewarding. Besides, your social life was not meant to be spent talking about your weekend over the water cooler. It was meant to be sweet-talking a cute girl while salsa dancing on the dance floor.

Better Family Life and Children – You could be that couple down the street. The high-powered investment banker and his non-profit lawyer wife. Both driving brand new high-end imports, always on the go, shuffling their kids to the latest hockey practice or dance recital. Both having to work to put their kids through private school and day care, not to mention make the mortgage payment on that McMansion they bought at the peak.

You could be that couple.

But you're not.

You're the single-income family where one of the spouses stays at home and raises the children. Packs them off to school. Helps them with their homework. You can't afford to take the kids to Europe like the couple down the street, but that's alright. The kids really loved the Black Hills and Mount Rushmore. And you can't afford dance lessons, but you still dance with your daughter in the basement using an instructional video you rented and some MP3's. You don't lease the newest Lexus, but you own that reliable used Ford free and clear. And when your spouse comes home you all have dinner, watch your favorite TV show, and maybe the Mrs. pours the hubby an adult beverage as the kids go to sleep.

No, you're not the couple down the street, but you're thankful for it. Because your spouse doesn't cheat on you. Your kids aren't in rehab. Your daughter isn't pregnant. Your house isn't in being foreclosed on. And you know and love your family. All because minimalism made it possible for you to spend time with them.

A Better Intellectual Life – It wasn't until I was older in life did I appreciate more intellectual things. School was so boring and the teachers so lacking in genuine intelligence and interest, it drove me (and millions of other young kids) screaming for home to play video games and watch cartoons. Because most teachers were so poor and so inept, they left a bad taste in most people's mouths when it came to education and expanding one's mind. However, this is a tragedy because one of the most enjoyable life experiences a person can have is expanding the mind and engaging in intellectual pursuits.

Good conversation, debate, studying history, pursuing new hobbies or studies, philosophy, talk radio, mathematics, etc., a limitless treasure of knowledge, thought and intellectual challenge is out there for everybody to avail.

Unfortunately, after 13 years of K-12 faux-education and an additional four years of collegiate brainwashing most people's minds are mush. And instead of getting a respite, allowing their brains to recover from nearly two decades of abuse, they simply plug themselves into the corporate machine, working a job that further liquefies their minds. At the end of the day when they're finally released from their mental prison, their brains are not dying to consume the works of Plato or learn another language. They just want to sit down, do nothing and veg out watching reality TV shows. The death of the mind is arguably the highest price corporate cogs pay. You needn't suffer that.

In pursuing minimalism you will have more free time to not just pursue physical pursuits, but mental ones as well. Reading, watching documentaries, whatever your brain desires and is curious about. Also, we are incredibly lucky today in that we have the internet. Not only is the information and knowledge available to us limitless, we now can engage and discuss with billions of other people about billions of different things. Yes, you may only be making $13,000 a year, but instead of spending 10 hours looking at spreadsheets or correcting computer code, you are on the internet debating the merits of Keynesian vs. Austrian economic thought, researching German weaponry of WWII, or watching the genius of Victor Borge.

Less Anger - One of the most enraging things that would get my blood boiling was watching immigrants who came to this country, not speaking a lick of English, buy their groceries with their EBT card. Similarly enraging was having the local WIC office located across the street from my office during my Wyoming days. Every day around lunchtime I got to see single mother after single mother go in there with three or four kids, all obese and certainly not lacking any food, rendering the first two hours of my day nothing more than slaving away for them.

Most Real Americans are angry. And they have every right to be. But once again, we must deal with "what is." It is a fact that immigrants will continue to come here and live off of our work. It is a fact that dumb, fat, trailer trash females will continue to spread their legs for their boyfriends and we will pay for their stupidity. And it is a fact naïve Americans will continue to vote for this. Don't get mad, get even.

In making only $15,000 a year you are essentially shrinking yourself (the host) so much that parasites cannot live off of you. Your federal tax rate is only 15% and with the standard deduction you'll only be taxed on about $9,000 in income. So your final tax bill is $1,350. Not only is it very likely you consume that yourself in public goods, you will probably get various refunds and tax credits like "Making Work Pay" lowering your final tax bill further. In short, nobody is living off of you. You have jettisoned the parasites.

Getting rid of the parasites and knowing you are no longer paying for them is quite a liberating feeling. You will no longer get mad when you see another ringless mother buying diapers with an EBT card. You will no longer care when the local school district demands more money. You won't even sneeze when they talk about the national debt. It's no longer your money they using to pay for it. It's somebody else's. You may still be unhappy about the general direction of the country, but at least you're no longer a sucker who has to pay for it.

More Travel – The primary reason people can't travel is not money. It's time. They don't have enough vacation time. But you will with your new minimalism lifestyle. The quality of your vacations will also improve. They won't be those "rushing vacations" where you race to every tourist trap, never get to take in any of the culture, let alone actually enjoy the vacation. No, you're going to be sitting in that Italian village on the Mediterranean for at least a week. May never leave the wine bar. Just sitting and looking at the sea. Maybe you'll go to the other wine bar down the street….nah…that would take too much effort.

Sleep – While people are suffering their daily two-hour commute, racing towards a stroke at age 47, you'll be sleeping in. Though, if you wake up early, you can do what I do - drive down to the local over-pass, light up a cigar and watch people suffer their Monday morning traffic jam.

Higher Chance of Becoming Rich – Counterintuitive as it may sound, you stand a much higher chance at becoming rich pursuing minimalism as opposed to slaving away for an employer. The reason is two-fold. First, it's nearly impossible to become rich working for somebody else. Understand while you can be promoted and make more money, the nature of your employer is to maximize profits for the owner, not you. This puts your self-interests in direct opposition to that of the owner. Not that this is evil or bad on anyone's part, it just is how it is. So there will always be that force keeping your salary as low as possible. And given the all the unemployed people more than happy to take your job, your employer can deliver that threat.

Second, most rich people are unique, not conformists. Nothing against your average corporate cubicle slave, but they lack the audacity and innovation to think beyond getting promoted to *assistant project manager*. Furthermore, they don't have the time to dream up or concoct business ideas. They work a boring job, the duties of which kill any innovation, and by the time they get home they just want to veg not develop a new product.

Now not that you were planning on starting the next Microsoft, but in pursuing minimalism you are already individualistic enough to have an entrepreneurial streak. You are also independent minded enough you will probably not let yourself sit idle. So chances are you will start tinkering with a hobby or a craft that you have a passion for, come up with an idea, and BOOM! Unbeknownst to you and quite unintentionally, you developed a business idea that would take off. It could be new way to breed wiener dogs, a new best-selling book, a better way to polish wood, whatever it is, your passion stands a better shot at making you rich than being a good, little loyal employee.

***

When you weigh the benefits of a minimalist life against the conventional, modern day American life, there really is no comparison. The benefits of the traditional American life are just not worth the price, let alone the risk. From an employment standpoint you are asked to give up nearly all of your youth pursuing degrees and certifications, with no guarantee of employment in return. Even if you do find employment, the labor market is so bad it has given employers a superiority complex, making most jobs insufferable and psychologically damaging. And even if you do manage to survive such a hostile environment with your sanity intact, the state is bound to be taking more and more of your money. Minimalism not only frees you from being dependent upon such a system, it delivers benefits that exceed any amount of money you could make as a working slave. You are allowed to live and enjoy life to its maximum potential, as well as develop yourself to your maximum human potential. You maximize the percentage of your finite life spent on leisure instead of labor. It's practically guaranteed you will lead a more interesting and rewarding life. And, ironically, even though you are trying to make as little money as possible, your chances of becoming rich are infinitely higher. In the end minimalism makes enjoying the decline more fun than if your wildest dream of winning the rat race had come true.

CHAPTER 4
MORTAL

*"Live life
like you're gonna die,
because you're gonna."*
-William Shatner

Whether you're pursuing minimalism, making psychological adaptations, or making behavioral changes in response to the decline, there should be an overarching principle or theory governing your decisions. And while giving you specific advice on buying motorcycles, getting rid of your stuff, eloping, etc., certainly helps, it won't address every problem or challenge you'll face in your life. Therefore it is better to understand a simple philosophy that will guide you throughout the rest of your life and that philosophy is one of mortality.

You are going to die.

Understanding and accepting death is the key to maximizing and getting the most out of your life. The amount of time you have on this planet is finite, it is precious, and only until you realize this will you be able to go out and truly enjoy the decline. Sadly, most people do not consider their finiteness until they are on the verge of death or the vast majority of their lives have been lived. Achieving nothing spectacular or particularly interesting, it is too late for them usually because they are too old, too frail, and too weak to go and reap the benefits life had to offer them. But worse still are people who are young, but let things outside of their control ruin their otherwise perfectly good lives, not to mention their futures. Therefore, if there is a psychological adaptation that has to be made to enjoy the decline, it is understanding you will die.

Since you are going to die, you now have to figure out what to do with your life. And while I personally can't tell you what that is, understanding the basic tenets of death and mortality will certainly provide you the perspective you need to make some wise decisions.

Tenet #1 - Underestimating Death – Most people have no idea what being dead is like, simply because nobody has come back from the dead to report their findings to us. However, a good proxy is what was it like before you were born? Do you remember anything before you were born? No? Then that's a pretty good indication of what it will be like after you die. Nothingness. An absolute absence of thought, consciousness, awareness, memory, or existence. It won't be painful or unpleasant. It just won't be. Yes, various religions have theories about an afterlife, but it is probably more likely you will merely cease to exist.

The problem is most people never give that concept the thought and pondering it really deserves. Right now, no matter how sucky your life, you get to wake up every day and think, feel, see, and touch. It's a movie being played in front of your very eyes where you are the main actor. It may not be the best movie, but it's your movie and you get to do whatever you want in it. When this movie is over, there is no more getting up, having coffee, talking to your loved ones, stubbing your toes, getting drunk, hitting your thumb with a hammer or the millions of other stimulations your brain receives every day. It's over. You will cease to exist. But the real loss is that you will no longer even be aware of yourself. You won't remember this moment reading this book. You won't remember your past. You won't remember the greatest moment in your life, simply because you won't exist. Again, nothingness.

This should be the 12 cylinder engine of inspiration (and even fear) driving you to live life to its fullest. It should be the epiphany that makes you stop doing the same damn, boring crap you do every day and start doing what you want before it's too late. Whether or not there's an afterlife is for another debate. The time you have now is the only thing you have. You MUST maximize it.

Tenet #2 – You Come First – Since this is your life you must lead it in a manner that benefits you the most. Of course, this does not mean you live your life at the expense of others or engage in criminal activity. And it doesn't mean you don't put loved ones ahead of you in that is arguably the definition of love. But you don't pointlessly submit yourself to anybody else unless that somehow benefits you. You don't slave away for other people without some reward (financial or emotional). You make sure every action in some way benefits you or the people you love. You make sure you get to live your dreams or die trying.

This is difficult in modern day America in that society is geared to be more communal than it is individualistic. Our tax rates are progressive, you are expected to be "honored" or "thankful" for having a job (when nobody asks why the employer shouldn't be "honored" and "thankful" for having your labor), you are expected to pay for other children's rearing and education, you are expected to pay for other people's lives. People's feelings and emotions trump your own. It is not an individualistic society.

Worse still, society LOATHES the true individual. Understand most people are brainwashed to be mediocre and forgettable. They are told to go to college, get a career, start a family, work 9-5, save up for retirement, live in Florida and die into obscurity. So when they see somebody living a different life, bucking the trend, and likely living a better life, they get incredibly jealous.

You don't want to have kids and prefer a life of luxury?

Why you're "selfish" and "greedy" for not ~~suffering like the rest of us~~ helping maintain the population.

Dare to be a bachelor past the age of 35, starting a company, and living a playboy lifestyle?

You need to stop being a man-child and start ~~marrying all those single moms who wouldn't give you the time of day in college~~ "manning up."

Are you financially successful, starting your own business?

You ~~better give me some of your money because I'm too lazy to work for it and will rationalize my stealing your money from you by citing things like "white privilege" and sexism~~ benefited unfairly and need to share.

You must ignore this social backlash and not let anybody pressure or intimidate you into doing something you don't want to do. It is your life, nobody else's. You live your dream.

Tenet #3 – Do Not Waste Your Youth - Whether you are aware of this or not, society is designed to waste your youth. Yes, people will spew platitudes like "the children are our future" or "won't somebody please think of the children," but they say that simply because they're taking advantage of younger people for their own personal gain. The perfect example is school.

Already at the age of 5 adults are lining up to live off of you. Oh sure they claim they're "doing it for the children" or "they want to work with children," but if you look at anybody who declares an education major you'll see the real reason they're doing it is for themselves. It's an easy job, it's an easy major, it requires no academic rigor or skill. Not to mention, if you ask the average 20 year old why they're majoring in education, more often than not they'll say,

"I get summers off."

It's definitely not for the children.

This also goes a long way in explaining why school is so dreadfully boring. If teachers really became teachers because they cared about children, then they would put the work and effort into making education interesting and beneficial to the children. They wouldn't just have a passion, but an expertise in the subjects they teach. They would major in engineering or math or biology, get experience in the real world and THEN teach. Not simply major in something as generic as "education," teach from the book, and wonder why their students are falling asleep in class.

Are there good teachers who have this passion and truly do care about their students?

Of course.

But if you take the time to count the number of teachers that were truly exceptional and taught you something, chances are you could count them on one hand (whereas you will roughly have about 83 teachers during K-College education).

The end result for children is they spend, at minimum, 13 years in a mental prison *for the benefit of others.* They learn nothing, their brains are destroyed, any raw talent or aptitude they may have had is quickly squashed by the mediocrity of their teachers, and when they finally graduate they operate at a mere fraction of their intellectual potential. All because a bunch of talentless charlatans wanted to become overpaid babysitters and had no moral problems abusing children in doing so.

If you still don't believe society is designed to parasite off of its youth, you just have to look at the next logical step in the career of a child – college. After graduating from high school every youth is practically commanded by society to attend college. But at least with K-12 education the child was not required to pay tuition. Now they are. And the price is steep.

College is merely a repeat of K-12 education. Most professors and academians didn't become teachers because of anything as "noble" as educating the children. They did it because teaching was easy. They did it because nobody would hire them in the real world. They did it because they're incompetent and simply can't "do." But since they wasted eight years pursuing their "Doctorate in African-American Studies" or some equally worthless garbage, the hell if they aren't going to get some poor group of young students to pay for it.

In the end the average student indebts himself upwards of $50,000 to pay a group of adults to blather nonsense at them for four years. They in turn get a piece of paper citing they showed up to class and had a pulse. However, with no actual skills gained, youth quickly find out the only job they're qualified to work is as a barista. 17 years of "follow your heart and the money will follow," "any education is a good education," and "it doesn't matter what you major in, it will open doors," and it was nothing but a big, elaborate, purposeful scam to take advantage of the youth.

Unfortunately, the wasting of youth does not end with the completion of their education. Not by a long shot. For even if young people are lucky enough to get a job, they're still slaving away for an employer. An employer who couldn't care less about the interests and goals of the youth.

For example, ask yourself the question. Has any boss or older person ever helped you out, mentoring you, guiding you, teaching you the ropes? Was there anything like a training program or some kind of tutoring when you started a job? Dare I ask if anybody in the past two generations has ever been groomed for a leadership position by an older person? Or was it just some middle-aged moron sitting at his desk parroting phrases like,

"steep learning curve"
"must hit the ground running"
"I don't have time, figure it out yourself?"

Has any older person displayed any real leadership in your life, demonstrating they knew what they were talking about and thus you should follow them? Has any older person shared their knowledge and wisdom with you in an effort to make your life better than theirs?   Has any boss or manager ever invoked an ounce of loyalty to them or the corporation? Or were the majority of them a bunch of abusive, inept, incompetent, dishonest, and outright stupid "pointy haired boss" types?

The truth is most employers and bosses offer college graduates nothing that even comes close to a genuine career. They advertise it as such. They use euphemistic titles. They even outright lie on the job description to get you to sign up. But in the end it's just all the crap work the boss plain doesn't want to do. Work that can be done by any competent 6th grader. Doesn't matter how talented you are. Doesn't matter what you're capable of doing. Doesn't matter you could do the job better than the higher ups. You are the stooge that gets to do all the crap work nobody else wants to. The fact is you are younger and probably pretty naïve. Most employers know this and purposely take advantage of this, promising you opportunity, but delivering you a dead-end job. This is not only why you shouldn't intern, but the second your job proves not to be as advertised you just walk off the job, no notice.

Misleading job descriptions, gopher-level work, and refusing to train aside, there is one other major way employers take advantage of youth – requiring a college degree for every job no matter how menial. Here employers are merely forcing you to participate in the education racket. Does the job require a bachelor's degree? No. But they're going to force all you poor kids to unnecessarily spend four years of your youth and $50,000 of your money just to have a *chance* at getting the job.

Not a guarantee. *Just a chance.*

It is the epitome of hubris and arrogance on the part of employers to demand applicants jump through such an expensive and completely unnecessary hoop. All they do is further contribute to the education bubble, condone progressive credentialism, and ruin the financial lives of young people.

Finally, say you are one of the lucky youth to land a job. Let's also say you are incredibly lucky to have a job that doesn't suck. You work hard, you make a lot of money, and your career is going great. Congratulations! You get to pay for...

Social Security and Medicare.

If there is proof society is designed to take advantage of and live off of its youth, Social Security and Medicare is it. Old people who didn't save up enough of their own money (not to mention, voted in politicians to blow all the money they did contribute away on social programs) effectively makes Social Security and Medicare Ponzi schemes. Their money is long gone, spent long ago. Retirees now rely on the young to work and pay the taxes to support them. Thankfully, our education system fails miserably at teaching our youth about public finances and the federal budget, so what they don't know won't hurt them. Furthermore, the education system does a spectacular job at brainwashing children, resulting in "youthful idiots" who unconsciously vote against their own financial self-interests (arguably the pinnacle achievement in abusing our children).

So with all these things stacked up against you, how exactly does one "not waste" their youth? You're forced to go to school for 13 years. The labor market practically forces you to get a college degree you won't use and don't need. And if you want food on the table you will have to work, thereby paying for the Social Security and Medicare of others. Epiphanies about being mortal aside, what's a young person to do?

It's very simple. Don't try until you're 35.

I've dispensed this advice many times before and it rings true today more than ever. Do not try until you're 35. The reasons are many. First, nobody takes you seriously until you're 35. You could be the top graduate in your class with internships under your belt and the perfect resume. Unless you have some gray hair, nobody is going to challenge you or give you a job that uses your skills. The reason why is because most youth suffer the reputation of their generation. So when an employer sees OWS protestors defecating on a police car or hipsters being...well...hipsters, they will unfairly lump you in with that crowd. So work all you want, get as many degrees as you want, and put in all those extra hours at the office, it will all be in vain. Wait until that work will go noticed. Wait until you have that "touch of gray."

Second, since nobody is going to take you seriously, you might as well remain a kid. So become a "ski bum." Not that you become an actual "ski bum," but you become whatever variant of "bum" you want to be. A "video game bum," a "motorcycle bum," a "travel bum," whatever it is you want to do. This doesn't mean you don't work, but (as per The Art of Minimalism) you work just enough to get by and play. Also, this is the stage of your life to pursue whatever great adventures you want. Driving to Cape Horn, biking around Europe, climbing Mt. Kilimanjaro, attending the Sturgis Rally. Whatever it is, do it now, because a lot of you won't be able to when you're 55.

Third, like there were jobs for you out there anyway. Not only are you purposely minimizing work to avoid paying taxes and save your youth, but barring some kind of economic miracle (or a bubble) you can expect your employment prospects to be on par with that of the Great Depression. Not only will this save you years of your time applying for jobs you're never going to get, this should assuage any guilt you have for being a "video game bum" instead of a CPA. Besides, what? Some employer was just around the corner about to offer you a *successful career*? The unemployment rate for youth proves there are no such opportunities.

Finally, since most of the education system is a scam, why waste your time in the system? Try to minimize the amount of time you spend in it. Not just college, but K-12 as well. If there is a way for you to become some kind of home-schooled wunderkind and graduate from high school at the age of 12, then do it. It will free up more of your youth to enjoy. Also, until a job, the economy, or your own personal intellectual interest warrants it, there's no reason to waste your precious youth earning a four year degree. Instead learn a trade you can carry with you wherever your "motorcycle bumming lifestyle" takes you. It will make earning money a little easier, allow you to find employment anywhere in the world, and it will be a lot better than living in your parents' basement.

Tenet #4 – Life is Too Short for Anger

Anger is a natural and necessary emotion in life. Though the left and society has tried its best to eliminate it or outlaw it, the fact still remains there are good reasons and appropriate times to get angry. When you or a loved one is threatened, when somebody is lying or trying to scam you, or when liberals tell you there's something wrong with you because you're angry. It is also completely acceptable to be angry over the current state of affairs in the United States. The problem is what does that get you?

Unless you can control the situation (say you are being attacked and need to fend off the assailant) your anger, no matter how justified, no matter how legitimate, is just wasted energy. Inevitably, you need to just let it go and not be angry anymore. This is very hard to do when your entire economic, political, and social environment is going to negatively affect your personal life. But again, the hard-to-learn skill of accepting what you do and do not control must be mastered in order to lead the happiest life.

The consequences of NOT learning this skill and letting anger get the best of you is that it will ruin your life. We all know these people. People who, if you were asked to describe the person, you would say, "he's an angry person." Where anger isn't a fleeting emotion, but is part of the person's permanent personality. Since anger is part of who they are, they're constantly in an angry state. And being in a "constantly angry state" precludes them of ever enjoying happiness. And while we may know "a person" that fits this description, the perfect example we can all learn from is your typical feminist.

For the most part feminism has won every societal, sociological, economic, and political battle in the United States. By all measures and accounts, feminism has won. But have you ever seen a "happy feminist?"

The reason they're not happy is because feminism has failed to win the one battle that is outside of their control – sexual nature. Namely the fact men like well-endowed, skinny women and women like strong, chiseled men. However, in refusing to accept the biological realities of men and women they condemn themselves to failure. Consequently, they get angry, and their lives are miserable.

But mock and ridicule feminism and feminists all we like, Real Americans run the risk of repeating the exact same mistake – getting angry over something outside our control, namely the collapse of the United States. Again, because it affects us so personally and we have such an attachment and love for the country, it is really hard to "just let go." But it's something we must do (akin to the 5 stages of grief) in order to move on with our lives.

To help, I recommend practicing an experiment I've found to be quite useful. Listen to the Ed Schulz Show or Rachel Maddow's show and try not to get angry. Listen to their willful ignorance, their intellectual dishonesty, the painful stupidity of their callers, and then see if you can let it go. This is a good practice in that it forces you into a situation you do not control, but by all means should be enraging. So if you can realize your reaction will have no effect on Ed or Rachel, let alone their hopeless callers, you will train yourself to react in the most healthy way possible – shaking your head and laughing. Not that I'd recommend becoming a regular listener (in that it would lead to depression and suicide), but if you can stomach such blatant lies and propaganda and *not* get enraged you will have learned a skill that will lead to a happier life (besides, look at just how "happy" Ed and Rachel are).

Tenet #5 – Carpe Diem

Standard in lessons about "you are going to die" is the advice of "seize the day" or carpe diem. Normally this entails something along the lines of taking chances, asking that boy out, starting that business you always wanted, etc. etc.

However, as evidenced by the majority of people's behavior, the vast majority of people might be aware of this advice, but rarely act on it. Very few people lead interesting or different lives. And regardless of how many people say, "they're independent" or they "do their own thing" most people end up living boring lives that are materially no different than vast majority of other people. So the issue is not one of understanding the concept of "carpe diem" it's an issue of taking action.

It is here we must live by the wise words of Butch Cassidy,

"Next time I say 'Let's go someplace like Bolivia,' let's GO someplace like Bolivia!"

All your dreams mean nothing unless you pull the trigger.

CHAPTER 5
FAMILY AND FRIENDS

"I have introduced myself. You have introduced yourself. This is a very good conversation."
-Katsumoto/"The Last Samurai"

With a thorough understanding of what is happening to our country, we need to turn our focus from acceptance and adaptation to one of enjoying life and enjoying the decline. Because no matter how bad things are and no matter how bad things are going to get, we still need to make the most of it. To do this we need to sit and ponder what really matters in life. What is most important in our lives. What is going to bring us the most amount of happiness. Thankfully the answer is quite simple and not up for debate.

Other humans.

Some people will disagree. Some will say riches, some will say wealth, some will say health, but those are all wrong answers. The correct answer is "other humans." The reason why is that out of *everything* on this planet, humans are the most interesting, entertaining, dynamic and intellectual things we'll ever run into.

For example, have the most advanced video-gaming system out there. It is still finite. It is still non-sentient. It cannot think, it cannot challenge you, and cannot engage you beyond what it is programmed to do. It is limited. The only reason it CAN challenge you to the extent that it does is because OTHER HUMANS programmed it that way. Furthermore, what do most people with video games do to maximize their fun? They go online and PLAY AGAINST OTHER HUMANS, suggesting it is human interaction, not a pre-programmed pixelated campaign to kill Nazi's or zombies that provides genuine stimulation to people.

Another example - when do you cry? Chances are when you crash your car or total your motorcycle, etc., you don't cry as much as you get angry. But when a family member or a loved one dies, you cry. Why? Because a human is the only thing you can really love, as well as love you back. It's the only thing that can interact with you. You could even make the same case for pets in that pets, though not as advanced as humans, have some of the same characteristics. They are not finite, they are not programmed, dogs certainly have personalities, they are dynamic (meaning they don't do the same thing over and over again like a robot), and you can interact with them. A Ferrari, you can't.

In other words, have all the things you want. Super computers, sports cars, European trips, an awesome career, you name it, there is nothing more advanced and engaging than another human being. It's what we're programmed to respond to. It's what we're programmed to be intellectually stimulated by. Other humans are the most important thing in our lives.

This is great news in that the largest threats facing all Real Americans are not social, but rather political and economic. The government may be able to take away your money, but it can't take away your friends. The government may be able to destroy the labor market, but it can't stop your children from hugging you. And the government may be able to force you to work until you're dead, but it can't stop somebody from loving you. In other words, take away all material wealth and economic opportunity, the government cannot take away the one thing that makes life worth living – human interaction.

Furthermore, in punishing work and production, the government is practically condoning your spending more time with friends and loved ones. If there are no jobs available, then that only means more cigar-smoking time with the guys at the cigar lounge. If putting in extra hours results being taxed at the 91% marginal tax rate, then that only means going home early and spending time with your family. And if regulations are going to prevent you from starting that motorcycle company, then heading out on a road trip with friends is a far better option.

But while government policy may inadvertently result in more time being spent with family and loved ones, that isn't to say the economic and political problems of the country won't stress our relationships. These external pressures will take a toll on our relationships with other humans. Thus, since our relationships with other humans are so valuable, we want to make sure we do our best to cultivate, optimize, and cherish our relationships especially within the context of the decline.

Friends

What makes friends arguably the most important people in your life, is that they don't *have to* hang out with you. They *choose to* hang out with you. Unlike the family you were born into, your friends aren't "honor-bound" by blood or social mores requiring them to spend time with you. They consciously decide to spend some of their finite, precious time with you. That's not only a great thing, that's a very humbling thing. Out of everything in the world those people could be doing, out of everybody in the world they could be hanging out with, for whatever reason they consciously and purposely chose you over all those other things. This is why you should not only be incredibly grateful for your friends, but why they should play a pivotal role in your life. Because without friends, your life is quite hollow, which is all the more reason we need to learn how to appreciate them and incorporate them into our lives.

First, realize how unique and personalized your friends are. While you can't pick your family, you can pick your friends. This effectively makes them your own "personally built family." It also makes them the most important thing you'll ever build. Some people will cite their careers or their reputations as the most important things they've built, when in reality it is your family of friends that is most important. These are the people who will account for the majority of your happiness, the people you will spend the plurality of your free time with, and the people who will give your life meaning. Additionally, since your "family of friends" is your own creation, the quality and caliber of those friends will speak volumes about you. Do you want to hang out with druggies, abusers, crusaders, and liberals? Or would you rather hang out with hard workers, self-reliant individuals, independent thinkers, and accomplished people? Life is too short to be surrounded by inferior people.

Second, because your friends are vetted by you, that means they like you. Sadly, the same cannot be said about everybody's family. A lot of people were brought into the world unwanted or unprepared for. Poverty, unexpected costs, abuse, divorce, or just plain immaturity on the part of ill-prepared parents has resulted in a lot of dysfunctional families and a lot of unloved people. Thankfully, just because the first 18 years of your life may not have been enjoyable, doesn't mean you have to suffer the remainder of your life. No matter how bad your family was, your friends are no doubt going to be much better. By definition they care about you. They will give you the hope and happiness that may have been missing in your past. More importantly they give you a future to live for.

Third, your friends are most likely going to be the single largest source of intellectual stimulation and engagement in your life.

Located in Roseville, Minnesota is a rundown strip mall. Every Sunday two of my friends and I would sit outside, light up cigars, and smoke.

Was the scenery particularly pretty? No, it was a parking lot of a rundown strip mall.

Were the girls particularly attractive? No, most of it was muffin top ghetto trash with too much make-up on, replete with illegitimate kids in tow.

Were the restaurants at least good? No, the food was quite average. We would only smoke, maybe purchase a soda, but rarely food.

So why would we select that place to smoke cigars? No reason at all. We just enjoyed talking to each other.

So stimulating was the conversation it didn't matter what environment we were in. Ghetto girls, WIC kids, crappy food, loud traffic. It certainly wasn't sitting at Lake Como in the Italian Alps. But that didn't matter. We were coming up with new, interesting and intriguing observations. Having epiphanies and philosophizing about different things. Challenging and questioning each other, making everybody think, pushing our minds to new frontiers. That was the pay off. That was the reason for being there – interesting and quality conversation. And while having fun and hanging out with friends is certainly enjoyable, it is quality conversation that makes a quality friend.

Ultimately, the role your friends will play in your life is the role of surrogate family to get you from the family you were born into, to the family you will inevitably start. And even then, it's not like your family of friends goes away. Your friends will start families of their own. Your families will play together and enjoy each other's company. And even if you don't start a biological family of your own, your family of friends will be there until you die. The single worst thing you can do, however, is "divorce" your family of friends. These are the people who are desperate to fall in love and the nanosecond they find somebody, POOF! They abandon their friends, never to be seen or heard from again...until they're dumped or divorced and sheepishly come crawling back. Do not be that person. Your friends deserve better. Besides, *"the marriage may come and go, but the [poker] game must go on."*

Family

Inevitably, no matter what you say, no matter how much you contend otherwise, you'll all become a bunch of Judases and betray your "family of friends." You and your friends will be having a grand ole time. You will have no responsibilities, you'll be whooping it up every night, you'll be dancing and drinking and playing video games, going to Vegas, having the best times of your lives. Of course *that* can't go on forever, so naturally, you'll choose to ruin all this fun by falling in love and getting married.

Of course I'm joking a bit, but compare and contrast the single, childless lifestyle versus that of starting and raising a family. The first thing you'll notice is that one is relatively risk free and the other is full of risk. Matter of fact, starting a family is most likely going to be the riskiest thing you do in your life. There are financial risks in that now you are responsible to feed, clothe and house your family members. There are legal risks in that if you and your spouse do not see eye to eye it will likely end up in divorce. And there are emotional risks in that if you and your spouse fail at marriage, your relationship and your children will suffer. All of this in the context of a decaying economic environment which is bound to put stress on you and your family. Given the prevalence of divorce, this requires blunt, forthright and truthful talk about the risks and responsibilities people have when it comes to raising a family. For while a family can be the most rewarding experience in a person's life, if done wrong it can be the bane of your existence.

***

The Husband's Responsibilities

#1 Choose a Good Wife

Of all the family members the husband has the most responsibility simply because it is the man who decides who he is going to marry and start a family with. Advances in feminism aside, women are still too cowardly to propose to men, thus leaving the first and most important decision about starting a family to the man – who will I start this family with?

Much as we might like to blame feminism for the decay in marital relations it is still men who day in, after day out, propose to these women only to end up with a 50% divorce rate. Admittedly, feminism has degraded the quality and caliber of women to the point most are unmarriageable, but that doesn't mean you "settle for what you can get," bringing children into this world with an inferior and inadequate woman. You must choose wisely, not just for any future-would-be-children's sakes, but for your own personal sake.

Sadly, making any kind of list or protocol on how to go about choosing a good woman is impossible. Everybody is different. Everyone has different tastes. No list fits all. But there are some very basic requirements or rules you can follow that will apply to everyone and lower the risk of choosing the wrong woman.

1. "It's not if you can live with her, it's if you can't live without her." If you don't feel compelled to propose to the girl, then she is not it. You need to need her.
2. Kindness trumps intelligence. I don't care how "intelligent" the girl is, if she isn't nice, it won't matter. You need a wife that likes you and is kind to you.
3. The most important thing in her life is you.

Unfortunately, while the above rules are simple and certainly true, they are idealistic. They assume you're dealing with a population of women circa 1946 - sane, rational, well-brought-up women who more or less have the same goals you do. This certainly is not the case today and thus this advice does not speak to the dating-market realities of modern western civilization. So while we'd all like to talk about unicorns and flowers and puppies and Oprah, I also believe some tough, cynical, street smart advice that has been forged at the front lines is merited as well. Specifically, red flags.

A Truly Independent Woman? - Does she support herself, or merely brag about how independent she is while she works as a part-time, non-profit charity counselor? You need a TRULY independent woman. Not a poser. Truly independent women do not brag about it, they just do it. While you may fashion yourself the majority bread winner of the family, there will come times (especially during the decline) when you'll need her to take the lead. If she is "faux-independent," living off your engineering salary as she pursues some "career" in creative writing, she will be unable to step up to the plate and help the family. She will invariably prove to be a liability, both financial and legal.

Her Major – Related to being independent, you want to find out how mature, adult, and realistic she is. What she declared as a major is very telling. If she's majoring in accounting, engineering, or getting her 2-year certification in welding, then that is a mature, responsible, adult woman who lives in the real world and is aware of the financial demands of independence. If she is 31, pursuing her third master's in "Social Work" with an undergrad in "Literature," not only is she still a child, mentally incapable of marriage, she is a financial risk never capable of producing the wealth necessary to support herself.

Her Politics - Specifically, what role does she see the government playing in your lives? If it's to be the provider of basic universal goods, legal systems, and defense, then fine. But if she believes the state should be the back-up provider for her and the children, then your role as a father and a husband is diminished and your authority over your own family compromised. Many young, modern day women prefer the financial security of a government check over that of a flesh and blood husband in that the government requires nothing of them in return and holds them to no standards. This relegates you to just a "social companion" and maybe a "sperm donor" to sire her children. You will not be the father or husband in this relationship. Just imagine being married to Sandra Fluke.

Problems with Sex and Intimacy - Women who do not like sex have something wrong with them. Something so wrong your primary concern should not be a sexless marriage, but what deeper, darker, more sinister underlying psychological problems she has. Women who have issues with sex are more likely to use it as a weapon or currency to extract resources from you. They will find anything sexual or physical "degrading" and berate you as "shallow" for having natural male tendencies. Also, women who dislike sex are more likely to claim sexual abuse. If the thought of a sexless marriage doesn't send you running, then trumped-up sexual abuse charges should.

Super Religious – Super religious women are not super religious because they believe in Jesus or anything as noble as that. They are super religious because they have screwed up in the past or are too weak to face reality and need some kind of psychological rationale to explain their failings. In other words, they abuse the religion for their own psychological purposes and really couldn't care less about Jesus. Religion also serves as the always available trump card allowing women to cite religion as a reason to do, or not do things. If they attend church that's one thing. If they start citing their religion as a reason they can't kiss you or why you can't date, don't convert. Run.

Where Is Daddy? – The best women I've ever dated all had one thing in common – they knew who their daddy was, dad was still around, and dad was still married to mom. The worst women I ever dated did not know their fathers and were raised by their mothers. Ask where daddy is and see if you can meet him.

Outsourcing the Children – Women who want to raise families and be a good wife want to *raise families and be a good wife*. That means either they or the father stays at home and actually *RAISES THE CHILDREN*. A woman who has no problem outsourcing their children to either pre-school, day care, or a nanny (as she is primarily concerned with returning to work) lacks the nurturing and caring instincts of a good wife and a mother. Additionally, it shows you she doesn't view other human beings (i.e.-her children) as sentient individuals that need care. She views them as consumer items that are to be consumed or purchased for consumption or status (think a luxury SUV). This means the child (and most likely the husband) are nothing more than "things" to have, not things to fall in love with. This is NOT to say women shouldn't work and should stay at home (as sometimes the father is best suited for child rearing). This IS to say a quality woman will at least ask the question,

"Well, who is going to stay at home and take care of the children?"

***

#2 Be "The Most Interesting Man in the World"

Criticize women all we may, modern day American men are not much better. They are overweight, they are effeminate, they have no drive, no desire to achieve, and they inspire nothing. Naturally, they themselves might be uninspired by the current vintage of modern day women, which may explain their current state. But if any of them want to find a woman who meets all the criteria above, they better dedicate themselves and their lives to attracting such a high-quality woman. Thus the goal when it comes to attracting a wife and making that wife happy is to become her very own "Most Interesting Man in the World."

If you look at "The Most Interesting Man in the World" he displays all the qualities and traits you should aspire to achieve. He is educated. Maybe not necessarily degreed, but he is able to carry on intelligent conversation, if not be the focal point of the conversation himself. He is also interesting, meaning different. He doesn't parrot what everybody else says, he doesn't aim to belong. He doesn't care. He does his own thing, has his own hobbies, and is living his life as he sees fit. He is mature, he is a man. He is not some fratboydouche with his hat on backwards saying, "hawt." Though he certainly doesn't submit himself to any woman, he is diplomatic, debonair, and charming to all women making sure to pay attention to them. He has a well-developed sense of humor, not slap stick, but dry and clever, vital to making the life of a woman much more rich and enjoyable.   Finally he is talented. He can tango, he can fix a motorcycle, he can read Arabic. He can do at least one thing nobody else in the world can, but most likely, more. He is "The Most Interesting Man in the World."

So how do you become "The Most Interesting Man in the World?" By improving every aspect of your life.

This means you have to develop a skill or a trade. This means you have to develop hobbies and interests that are not common, but still unique and interesting to you. This means you have to consider others and how you interact with them. It also means you must polish yourself, your actions, and your demeanor. You need to become well-read, well-informed and knowledgeable. And hardest of all you must develop charm and a devastating sense of humor that will turn your future wife's knees to rubber. When you walk into the room you want to be the most interesting man in the joint, not to make all the other women insanely jealous of your wife, but your wife insanely proud of you.

Of course, none of this can happen overnight. But like a fine scotch, in due time you will age to perfection. You just follow one simple rule – do your own thing – and you will invariably become your own version of "The Most Interesting Man in the World."

#3 Stay in Physical Shape

Though maintaining your physique would be implied in being "The Most Interesting Man in the World," I wanted to address it separately in that it is so important it warrants its own discussion.

While physical attraction is very important to men, it is assumed that is not the case with women. Unfortunately, that is a lie. Women may not value physical attraction as much as men, but they still value it. Additionally, if you have a mentally healthy wife, she will like sex, probably love it...probably to the point you'll be turning her down. So if you are going to demand your wife stays in physical shape, you owe it to her to do the same.

This means diet and daily exercise are MANDATORY regimens of the husband. Much as running is exhausting and boring, you must do it. As mind-numbing as lifting weights is, you must do it. And though you would love nothing more than to pig out on an all you can eat buffet of Mexican food, you can't. You need to be physically strong, physically fit, in shape and sexy. Your other option is to let yourself go, which will result in her letting herself go, and the sexless marriage that is guaranteed to ensue.

#4 Keep Your Nose Clean

One of the most insulting things men face today is the plethora of single mothers. Not so much that they exist, but that society has brainwashed them into thinking there's nothing wrong with being a single mom (or worse, they're somehow "heroic"). So when a childless, never-married man refuses to date or consider single mothers for marriage they are immediately eviscerated as uncaring, selfish, and sexist.

But let's turn the tables. Say you are the father of an illegitimate child. Or you married the wrong person and are now divorced. Are never-married, childless women supposed to ignore that? In truth, you know it's an insult to any woman you'd propose to in that you have another woman's child and were previously married to another woman. At minimum, you would acknowledge this lowers your market value as a potential spouse. The issue is not whether you should marry single parents, the issue is to make sure you don't become one in the first place.

You owe it to your future wife to keep your nose clean. This doesn't mean you go to church and never have sex, but you make damn sure you don't bring any illegitimate children into this world. This means you make sure the woman you marry is the "one and only" and not the first in a series. This also means you don't end up in jail, you don't file for bankruptcy, and other basic things. Additionally, forget becoming "The Most Interesting Man in the World." Do you have any idea how marketable you are if you are over 30 and:

1. Don't have kids
2. Never been married
3. Never been to jail
4. Don't live at home
5. Have a job?

In simply not botching up your life you'll already be well ahead of your competition, and that's without lifting a single weight or running a single mile. That's the absolute *least* you can do for your wife.

#5 Be a Male Role Model

The majority of society's problems you will find stem from the lack of fathers. This has been a direct consequence of feminism trying to eliminate the distinction between "fathers" and "mothers," and worse, marginalizing the role fathers play in the upbringing of children as "unnecessary." It is assumed that only a mother is needed to bring up a child, while the father's role is merely financial. Thankfully, to leftists anyway, that role is easily outsourced to the state.

The price paid, however, is not endured by the father or the mother, but rather the children they bring into this world. This is no more apparent than in the black community. With 70% of births being outside of wedlock, the majority of which results in an absent father, there is no paternal disciplinarian to enforce rules, obedience, but more importantly, a moral code. And while the state may come in and supplant the father in terms of his financial role, the state cannot come in and replace him in terms of his mentoring and leadership role. The results are obvious. Young black males (as well as females), without a father figure, commit more crime, perform worse academically, and suffer lesser lives because of it. The severity of the problems facing the black community should render accusations of racism moot. Besides, the same trend is happening to all races, it just happens to be the black community is furthest down this rabbit hole.

The larger point for all races is the importance of having fathers in children's lives. Without a father your children are going to go into the real world without knowing how to deal with ½ of society - men. Your daughters will have a heavily skewed biased towards their own self-importance, but worse a dangerously naïve understanding of men, men's sexual nature, and the risks those pose. Your boys will suffer as well. With no man to teach them the harsh realities of life such as competition, independence, self-reliance, self-control, and work ethic, boys will grow up woefully unprepared for the real world. Not just in terms of work ethic and skills, but they will have no clue how to interact and deal with women. Their lives will be failures, both financial and romantic, but worse they won't know why. With no leadership or guidance, you've left them to roam aimlessly for at least a decade, forcing them to figure it out on their own through trial and error. This will exact a heavy toll on their emotions and psychology, and that's assuming they are even successful in figuring it out for themselves, instead of living cluelessly for the rest of their lives.

It is here, men, for the benefit of yourself, but more importantly, your children you must ignore and refuse to abide by whatever societal and political pressures are put on you to NOT be a man and NOT teach your children in a manly way. Despite what society has told you, men do account for half of the population and we are equally important as any other group. Any loving father who cares about his children will prepare them for this reality through discipline, structure, and tough fatherly love. It is better to be a divorced father, who still is a man and educates his children as such, than a married man who is cowardly, spineless, and parents through compromise. In the end, your children will not only be happier, more successful, and mentally healthy, but thankful and likely to visit you in a nursing home.

***

The Wife's Responsibilities

#1 Choose a Good Husband

Just like a man owes it to himself and his future children to find a good wife, you owe it to yourself and your future children to find a good husband. And while the qualities and traits desired between men and women differ, the three general rules still apply:

1. "It's not if you can live with him, it's if you can't live without him." If he were to propose and you aren't sure, then he isn't the guy for you.
2. Kindness trumps intelligence. I don't care how "intelligent" he is, if he isn't nice, it won't matter. You need a husband that likes you and is kind to you.
3. The most important thing in his life is you.

Of course, again, this assumes you're courting the likes of Ward Cleaver or Jimmy Stewart. The quality of men has certainly deteriorated since then, requiring we take a look at some more modern, street smart advice.

Is He Abusive? – It doesn't matter if it's physical or mental, any abuse is unacceptable. I wish I didn't have to write this, but sadly a lot of you women just aren't getting the message. I've seen women physically abused and more often than not, mentally abused as well. What's worse is a lot of you girls take it when there are much better men out there for you. However, while you may not respect yourselves, at least be selfless enough to respect your children . Chances are if the guy is going to abuse you, he'll abuse children as well. And it's completely unacceptable to bring children into such an environment.

Is He an Independent Man? – An independent man is a real man. They are mentally stronger, more capable of dealing with problems, and more mature. He may not be a rich man, but a man who has had to support himself will prove to be a better husband and father. So while "Thadeus Winthrop IV" may have a six-figure job at the age of 26 at his daddy's company, chances are he's arrogant, self-centered, and incapable of dealing with real problems or emergencies. You want a man who has had the trials and tribulations in life to appreciate what really matters – you.

It Doesn't Matter How Much He Makes – While money is nice it is not the most important thing. Yes, you need some money to live, but he doesn't have to make six figures. Additionally, you may not have a choice. With the economy being as poor as it is and the public sector crowding out the private sector, men will take a disproportionate toll, likely making less money in the future. You have to ask yourself if money is more important than a loving husband. If that's the case "Thadeus Winthrop IV" might date you for a while before inevitably dumping you for a 23 year old floozy.

Does He Have Dreams? – A man without dreams is like a boat dead in the water. A man needs to have a goal or a mission in life to not only achieve some modicum of success, but also to define himself. It may seem odd, but men are genetically hard-wired that way. However, sometimes women fear men would put these goals ahead of them, putting the wife in second place. However, this is the wrong way to think about it. Without dreams a man is a shell. A depressing shell that is *likely to suck all the life out of you.* You want to find a man who is happy on his own pursuing his dreams. This means he will choose to spend his life with you because he wants to. Not because he doesn't have anything else to live for.

His Politics – The difference between the psychologies of liberal men and conservative/libertarian men is that of competition. Conservative men embrace competition. Liberal men avoid it. Conservative men want to achieve excellence. Liberal men want to achieve equality and fairness. What's interesting, though, is if you look at what drives men to reach these political beliefs, it's nothing as lofty as independent thought or conducting economic research. It's something much more Darwinistic – their looks.

To be blunt, the reason why liberal men are against competition is usually because they are uglier and weaker. Thus, it is in their best interests to have an egalitarian society where they don't have to compete. Consequently, better looking and stronger men favor free market ideologies because they can leverage their strength, looks, and tenacity to improve their lives. Most people will dismiss this as punditry and hogwash, but the empirical evidence is abundant. All one has to do is look into a bumper-sticker-laden hybrid car or the local organic grocery store and see if any of those guys are the types women want walking them home late at night.

The issue is not so much one of politics, as much as it is being honest with yourself. The vast majority of women, regardless of political ideology, want manly men. It's programmed into their DNA. And the worst thing you can do is let politics overrule your biology, and suffer a marriage to a scrawny, effeminate weakling you're not physically attracted to. Not only will you not be satisfied, your biology will win in the end and you will most likely cheat on him or divorce him. Do not let politics get in the way of nature.

His Humor – A man must be able to make you laugh. Whether it's slap stick or dry humor, life is too short to be with some guy who doesn't make you laugh. Additionally, men with a sense of humor make spectacularly better fathers than those who don't. Also, men who don't have a good sense of humor are likely to be one of those "angry people," constantly brooding, incapable of enjoying life. So don't worry so much about his pocket book or ask him what he does for a living. When you meet a guy at a bar, see if he can tell you a good joke.

***

#2 Other Men's Children Are Not Our Problem

Just like men, women can also torpedo their chances by bringing other men's children into this world. Despite what Hollywood tells you, despite what "The View" says, and despite what your women's magazine says, having another man's child is an insult to any man you will court in the future. This isn't to say no man will marry you, this isn't to say your child was a mistake, it is a factual statement that you may choose to ignore or accept.

The solution, again, is simply not to have illegitimate children or marry willy nilly in the first place. Keep your nose clean. And just like a man over 30 who's

1. Never been married
2. Doesn't have kids
3. Has a job and
4. Has managed to stay out of jail

has a huge competitive advantage over his peers, a woman with the same traits will command a premium as well.

#3 Kids Are Not Toys

When I heard the term "baby rabies" I had to laugh. The thought of a woman so desperate to have children she had become "rabid" was funny. However, there is a seed of truth in that phrase - some women want children so badly, they don't even care if they should be having children in the first place. Unfortunately, a woman doesn't have to be "rabid" about children to make the mistake. She just has to be the average American woman who's been brainwashed to believe she can "have it all," juggling a career, a family, and a husband.

The sad truth is that you cannot have it all. There is not enough time during the day to adequately tend to all three. The adage,

"Children, Husband, Career – choose two"

is not evil misogynist, patriarchs trying to keep you down. It's people who are older and wiser than you trying to prevent you from making a mistake and ruining your life.

This does not mean you can't have a career, but if you're going to bring children into this world, then *somebody* should stay home to raise them. If your career means that much, then your husband better be the one staying home taking care of the kids. But if you both demand a career and simply outsource the upbringing of your children to daycare or a nanny, then why did you have children in the first place? You obviously don't care about them. You obviously didn't have children for the sake of the children. You had them purely and greedily for the sake of you. i.e.- they're not human beings you wanted to bring into this world and spend time with raising. They are "things" you wanted to "own."

Fortunately, men are becoming aware of how important it is to have somebody stay home to raise the children. So when men see women decreeing "they will have a career and couldn't care less who raises their future children," it sends them running. Because if your career is more important than your children languishing in some daycare facility, that screams to the world,

"I'm more important than everybody else, including my children."

And good luck finding a husband with that.

#4 Kids Do Not Replace Your Husband

When you bring children into this world, your husband doesn't go away. He's still there. He is not some disposable thing that served a function, made a deposit, and now can be ignored. If you want a happy marriage, you better attend to him just the same. If you want a happy and successful family, you better make sure he's an integral part of it.

#5 Importance of the Division of Labor

The inane and life-long debate about men not doing enough chores around the house is a debate that should be killed, burned, dragged, spat upon, and buried in the ground forever. Not only do men typically do more maintenance and repairs, they are also usually in charge of the overall strategic planning of the family. They have to think about where to live, what is the economy doing, what to invest in, how are our finances, how do I position the family to benefit the most from our environment, etc., etc.

These chores go unnoticed because it keeps the ship running smoothly. Only when the man is not around or one of these things goes awry do the rest of the family members notice. However, since it isn't a "daily" chore like cleaning any work he does "behind the scenes" goes unnoticed. Sure enough, up comes the wife, nagging him to take out the garbage while lecturing him about how he doesn't do his "fair share."

If there is way to drive a man into the arms of a hotter, younger mistress it is failing to appreciate his efforts and the division of labor.

The "division of labor" is a simple economic law first noted by Adam Smith. In short, instead of having everybody do a little bit of everything, each person specializes in one task. Not only does production go up, but quality improves. This same economic law applies to a household.

Men, because of their strength, mathematical, and spatial recognition abilities are better at fixing things, repairing things, building things, and strategic planning. Women because of their strengths in compassion, thought, psychology, as well as their physical weakness are better suited for child-rearing, household chores, shopping (meaning budgeting and increasing the purchasing power of the family), etc. This is not to say a woman can't fix an engine. Nor is it to say a man cannot do the dishes. It is to say that men and women have different strengths and weaknesses which make them better and more productive at completing specific tasks which increases the overall standard of living the family gets to enjoy.

To make your family's life happier (not to mention, avoid driving your husband insane), you need to do two things. One, realize men have a lower standard of cleanliness than most women. We got by for 30 years being bachelors and never suffered infection, disease, or even a paper cut. Our bachelor pads were "clean enough." We will clean up to that level. If you want it cleaner, do it yourself. Two, do not violate the law of the division of labor. If he is already changing the oil, do not tell him he needs to clean the bathroom. If he has reviewed the quarterly 401k statement, do not lecture him about the dishes. And if he put a new filter in the furnace don't nag him about vacuuming.

Remember, Bambi the well-endowed 23 year old secretary is always there, waiting.

#6 Two Captains Sink a Ship

Ballroom dancing is the PERFECT model of a marriage. There is a man and a woman. Typically the man leads, the woman follows. However, regardless of the sex, one person HAS TO LEAD and the other person HAS TO FOLLOW. Ballroom dancing won't work if you have two leaders trying to tug each other around, just as it won't work if you have two followers just looking at each other waiting for the other to lead.

This binary relationship also applies to marriage. If you have a family, that means there can only be one head of the household. But just like ballroom dancing, if you have two leaders, or two followers, nothing gets done and the system collapses. Typically the men are the head of the household, so in the majority of instances you will be the follower (though, again, sometimes the women prove to be the better leader). So in order for it to work, that means you NEED TO FOLLOW.

Should you voice concerns? Of course.

Should you get your opinion in? Naturally.

But if you constantly question your husband, nag him, resist him, or try to lead, you will get the same results as in ballroom dancing - aggravation, anger, failure, arguing, yelling and the men just giving up (all of which I have witnessed in my ballroom dance classes). Realize being the follower is NOT a subservient role, it is a role equal to that of the leader. A ballroom dance cannot be held if there is no follower. But if there is, and she is a great follower, you can have a spectacular marriage just like a spectacular dance.

#7 Support, Do Not Nag

In line with the dynamics of leader/follower, most men are constantly working towards some larger goal. Financial stability, security, housing, whatever. And unless they're goofing off, there's a darn good reason they're doing the things they do. Additionally, their goal is to get it done as quickly as possible so they can go and enjoy their leisure time, namely with you and the kids. But you do him no service getting in there and questioning him or nagging him about what he is doing. If anything, you get in the way, you slow down his progress, and you frustrate and anger him.

It is akin to being a cyclist. Every cyclist knows that the best pavement to bike on is freshly laid asphalt. The primary reason is that it is smooth.

Since it is smooth there is less friction between the road and the tires, resulting in a faster speed, with less effort. The WORST type of pavement is the warning tracks where the road is purposefully grooved. Though those grooves may not seem like much, they can easily slow you down by 70% compared to a freshly paved road. Nagging is those grooves and has the exact same devastating and debilitating effect on your husband. Therefore, don't nag him, support him…that or just leave him alone.

#8 Stay in Shape

The single most important thing you can do for your man is stay in physical shape.

This is not politically incorrect.
This is not sexist.
This is not evil.
This is not shallow.

This is the truth. It is not optional. You have no choice in "accepting it." If you want to be lied to, listen to Oprah.

Physical attraction is more important to men than women in that sex is also more important to men than women. This doesn't mean he gets to be a slob, while you slave away working out four hours a day, but if you want a successful and happy marriage, you better stay in shape. This entails not just your physique, but your physical appearance as well. Heels, no matter how uncomfortable are an unfortunate consequence of a happy husband. Lingerie, better learn to love it. Sharp daily attire, you bet. You don't have to be a model every day, but if your husband isn't pawing at you at least once a week, then you are failing.

Additionally, the single biggest hurdle of maintaining your beauty will be weight control. This is a *"do or do not, there is no try"* responsibility. Unless you have a glandular problem (which only 5% of the population does) you plain have no excuse for being fat. It simply requires diet, exercise, and discipline. "Diet" meaning you strictly adhere to a diet. "Exercise" meaning you are sweating, not merely "going for a walk" or "jazzercising." And "discipline" meaning, "I'll have no cookies" instead of rationalizing, "Well I'll have four cookies instead of five."

Finally, do not use sex as a weapon or a currency simply because men desire sex more. Married or not, if you're holding out on him, a man has every right to leave you and find it somewhere else. And while you may not view that as moral and contend he doesn't have the "right," agreed. But he does have the ability. This doesn't mean every request has to go fulfilled, but if you knowingly and purposely are using sex to extract resources from him or punish him, then you might as well divorce him because that's where it's headed.

***

Children

Unless you really want them, I strongly advise against having children in that they can severely cripple your ability to enjoy the decline. Since the majority of problems you'll face will be economic and financial, cutting $250,000 per kid in expenses can make your life a lot easier. Even if you do want kids and believe they are necessary for you to lead a happy and fulfilling life, you have to ask yourself what kind of world are you bringing them into? Even more so, what kind of future are they likely to have? You have to be able to love your to-be-born kids enough to know and accept whether you should even be having them in the first place.

That being said, a lot of people really want children and cannot see living life without them. Additionally, the question is moot for the people who already have children. So given our current economic environment and the progressively dismal future what can you do to benefit your children the most and make sure they enjoy the decline as well?

This first thing you can do is not lie to them. This is arguably how we got into this mess in the first place - by lying to younger generations about the economic realities of the world. Yes, it's difficult being a parent, and yes it's difficult delivering bad news or playing the "bad cop," but simply ignoring these harsh realities won't make them go away. All you manage to do in not teaching your children the harsh lessons of the real world is outsource that task *to the real world*. And the real world is nowhere near as nice and compassionate as you are.

Additionally, kicking the can down the road is one thing. Your child will get a rude awakening when they graduate from college and face an unemployment rate of 15%. But you make that rude awakening even worse if you inflate the kid's ego and expectations of the future. If you tell a kid for 18 years of their life, "you can do whatever you want" or "follow your dreams and the money will follow" or other such poppycock, they will be crushed doubly so when they don't live up to the impossible expectations you MISLED them to have.

Ultimately what you need to do is parent, not be their BFF. You did not have children because you were bored or lonely. You had children because you wanted to raise them and start a family. Thus, as should be the goal of any parent, your goal should be to raise them to become functioning, independent, self-reliant adults. In other words, you're not raising them in fear of how they will judge your parenting ability today (thus driving modern day parents' desire to be "BFF's"), but rather in fear of how they will judge you when they are 30. Because it is then they will have the maturity, worldly experience, and hindsight to determine whether or not you did indeed do a good job parenting. And it is then they will decide whether or not to keep you in their lives.

Naturally, this isn't going to be all roses and wiener dogs. You will have to engage in the hated and much maligned art of "tough fatherly love." You'll need to discipline them, punish them, set boundaries, and other things that aren't pleasant. But most importantly you will have to train them for their future. It is here, that though I am not a parent, I can't believe my eyes. Of all the parents I know, none of them sit their kids down and talks about the future. None of them have heart to heart talks with their children. None of them take the time to impart the wisdom they've learned, so that their children have better, or at least easier lives than they do. It is here I believe modern day parents can do the most to help their children prepare for and enjoy the decline, not to mention learn some things themselves and have some bonding time with their children.

For example, most modern day parents are woefully inadequate when it comes to personal financial planning. Most families do not have budgets. Most families don't invest or save for emergencies. Most families just fly by the seat of their pants. But worse, even if families do budget, how many parents share this information with their children? Not only would it explain why the family can't go to Disney World every week, it would teach the young tyke some very important financial lessons; You can't spend more than you make, the concept of borrowing and debt, the concept of taxes, etc. Not only would you be doing your child a great service in preparing them for adulthood, you would lower the risk of him living at home at the age of 32.

Another area you can learn, bond, and prepare for the decline is economics and politics. Here, again, modern day parents are only tacitly aware of the country's finances, presenting another opportunity to learn together with their children. You can learn what makes a country rich, what makes a country poor, different variants of GDP, why different assets go up in value while others go down, all of which will lay the foundation for your child to make wise investments in the future, not to mention make wise decisions when it comes to pursuing a career.

Another way to help your child is to help them with their homework. No, not hire a nanny or a tutor. YOU help them with their homework. You do this not only to make sure your child gets good grades and will do better in school, but also for your own benefit to keep your mind sharp (do you remember trigonometry?), and show your child you care about them.

A fourth way to help your child is to teach them a skill or a trade. Namely, repair. I would have killed to have a father show me how to take apart an engine or change oil or clean a carburetor. I would have killed to have a father who'd show me how to sheet rock and how to roof. Sadly, most modern day fathers have lost these skills and trades as they've outsourced auto and home repair to professionals. But thanks to YouTube both you and the whole family (ma included) can teach yourselves how to align tires or replace a water pump or pour concrete. Furthermore, your child will not just benefit in that they'll learn a skill that will save them thousands in the future, but they will have learned the most important skill of all – how to self-teach.

Finally, don't forget to make their childhoods enjoyable. The risk you run in training them to be an adult all the time is that you forget this is their childhood. You need to make it fun. And not just fun, but memorable. Besides, if you don't take advantage of your kids being kids now, the opportunity will never return. The time to take that great American family vacation is when you have a family, not when all your children are on campuses strewn across the globe. The time to go to Disney World is when your children still want to, not when they're 28. And if you can't afford trips, it doesn't matter. More than anything else children want their parents to spend time with them. Baseball games, playing with them at home, whatever it is, those 18 years will go by fast and by then you will have forever lost the opportunity to play with your children.

You Are the Joneses

Regardless of what happens to the economy and the country, in focusing on the people in your life you will lead the richest life you possibly can. While people are knocking themselves out, working 60 hour work weeks just to have a "successful career," you'll be spending time with your friends enjoying life. When the neighbors are at their wits end dealing with their problem children, you'll be happy somebody stayed at home to raise yours. And while working out may be a chore, your sex life will be better, your chances of divorce lower, and you'll be the envy of all other married couples.   These things cannot be taken away by the government and is what you should focus on to enjoy the decline.

CHAPTER 6
CAREER AND EDUCATION

"I have never let my schooling interfere with my education."
-Mark Twain

An integral part of your life will be your career. Not only will it define you personally, it will also be the primary source of money used to finance your life. But in order to have a career you will need a certain amount of training or education. This makes what you choose to study arguably the most important financial decision in your life since it will have such a large and determining effect on your lifetime earnings and standards of living.

Historically, the education industry and corporate America have had a mutually beneficial relationship with the American people that helped serve all three parties in this regard. For the price of tuition the education industry would educate and train people, giving them the skills they needed to command a higher salary in the labor market. Employers in turn would hire this skilled labor, providing them with compensatory wages and some modicum of job security. Unfortunately this relationship has ended.

Today both of these institutions have become corrupted, no longer serving their original functions and, more often than not, taking advantage of the individual. The education industry has become nothing more than a scam, charging way more in tuition than what their degrees could ever possibly be worth. And employers, flush with a surplus of desperate labor, have become arrogant and condescending to the point job performance is no longer based on competency and kicking ass, but navigating office politics and kissing ass. The end result is the individual taking on all the financial risk of earning a degree, the risk he or she may never find a job, and even if they do, the employer has likely made the working environment so psychologically hostile it's impossible to have anything idealistic as a "rewarding career."

This puts the individual in a quandary. Everybody needs to have at least *some* kind of career, and in today's labor market, that means you have to get *some* kind of education. But with corporate America and the education industry so blatantly abusive of the individual, how do you navigate this minefield?

Craftily, of course.

The first thing to realize is that the current deal the education industry and American employers are offering you is completely unacceptable. As it stands right now employers are effectively ordering you to get a bachelor's degree, regardless of whether it's actually needed or not. The education industry knowing this, jacks up tuition while at the same time keeps touting the value of an education, no matter how worthless it truly is. Sadly, with everybody getting bachelor's degrees, the value of the degree drops, forcing people to get even more education (again, no matter how unnecessary) simply to distinguish themselves from their peers. So by the time you're 26 you finally graduate and are ready to hit the job market.

Unfortunately, without economic growth there are no jobs, forcing you to either accept a menial job, for which no degree is required, or continue on the path of progressive credentialism, earning licenses, certifications, and so on. Maybe, finally, around the age of 30 you are actually employed at a job that might be near your competency level. But at what cost? You've been in school since the age of 5. It "only" took 25 years of your youth, $100,000 in tuition and education, and many times more in taxpayer dollars to train you to the level where employers are FINALLY willing to hire you? That's not only unacceptable, that's insane.

Additionally, such a system makes it impossible for the average individual to live a life. If it takes 30 years to incubate labor, that leaves that individual with very little time to pursue life's other pursuits. You have to pay off your student loans, which pushes you to the age of 35. Then, if you want to start a family, you'll inevitably need a house, the mortgage of which pushes you to 65. Auto loans, credit card debts, and the miscellany of other debt you'll incur will put you past 70. And heaven help you if you were foolish enough to sign off on your children's student loans. You won't be debt free until you're 80.

Since this system isn't even possible, you have only one choice when it comes to dealing with the social contract employers and the education industry are offering – reject it. But that doesn't mean you walk down to the welfare office and start collecting a check. American employers and the education industry can still play an advantageous role in your career. The trick is to take advantage of them, not let them take advantage of you.

Make Them Work For You

Key to fully taking advantage of our current employer/education system is to divorce yourself from the idea that somehow there's a career out there for you. Despite what you've been told, you are not that special someone who will beat the unemployment rate odds, the sclerotic economic growth, and the other damning and compelling economic realities of this country. You are not going to become a successful "marketing executive." And just like everybody else, your employer will fire your ass in half a second if it results in an extra $4 in profit. This isn't to say there isn't a *chance* you might have a successful career, but it is to say the cost of pursuing something so improbable is too high – your life. If you pursue a career and it doesn't pay off, you have done nothing more than waste your youth and cripple your financial future. Again, don't try until you're 35.

In making a "career" no longer your primary goal in life, you'll manage to fundamentally change the relationship you're going to have with your employer. You don't need your employer for advancement. You don't need your employer for opportunities. You certainly don't need your employer for your livelihood. And you don't need your employer for happiness. The only thing you need your boss for is to get paid. Or in the wise words of Cpt. Malcolm Reynolds:

"So let me make this abundantly clear. I do the job and then I get paid."

In taking away all the ancillary reasons, as well as any desire for future with the company, you've taken the vast majority of power away from your boss. You don't need him anywhere near as much as he needs you. In other words, he is serving your needs, not the other way around.

But if your relationship with your employer has been minimized to the point you're only using him for money, what role can an employer play in your career?

Very simple. None.

Ideally, your employer will be financing you until you don't even need him. Not that you will have accumulated enough money to be independently wealthy, but you will have built up a business on the side, no longer requiring an employer at all.

In short, in order to truly enjoy the decline the ideal employment situation is one of self-employment. You will be spending 2,000 hours per year for about 50 years working for somebody, and it might as well be you. You are going to treat yourself better than any other boss out there. You are going to maximize your pay (whereas all bosses do the opposite). You will not abuse yourself. And it is most likely you will be pursuing something you have a passion for instead of the mind-melting work offered by most employers. You are merely using your employer as a temporary measure, to be discarded as quickly as possible.

What you decide to do for a living, however, is completely up to you. Obviously, if you wish to enjoy the decline, it should be something you enjoy and are passionate about. And of course it can't be something stupid like "horse farms" or "coffee shops" or other such profitless hobbies that only morons pursue. But whatever it is you ultimately decide to pursue, the hardest part about running your own business is simply pulling the trigger and doing it. It may not become apparent right away, and you may have to work a full decade before thinking up an idea or identifying a market. But when the opportunity does present itself you must take advantage of it.

Until that point in time there is plenty you can do to prepare. You can learn accounting, which is a MANDATORY skill if you're going to run your own business. You can learn about setting up LLC's, S-corps, C-corps and other form of businesses at your local secretary of state. You can take some introductory business courses (though beyond an introductory course is unnecessary). And you can learn how to draft up a business plan, which will become necessary should you need to approach a bank for financing. There is plenty of leg work to do in anticipation of starting your business, leg work that will only serve to help ensure its success.

Trades and Skills

Not everybody can be an entrepreneur, and thus, starting your own business may not be a viable option for you. However, you can still use employers and the education system to your advantage by pursuing different types of careers instead of the traditional bachelor's-degree-9-to-5 type professions. Namely, the trades.

The trades have elements of both traditional employment and the capacity for self-employment, the reason being that a trade is transferable and the person with the trade can offer his or her service without having to be employed by a company. For example a good friend of mine earned her dentistry degree. The school recommended that upon graduation students work under another dentist as a form of apprenticeship, to take what they learned in the classroom and apply it to the real world. However, this was not necessary. My friend, though a bit apprehensive about striking out on her own, decided to do precisely that. Not only was she incredibly profitable her first year, she saved herself at least a year in unnecessary apprenticeship.

Another benefit of the trades is that trade certification is a lot cheaper than earning a four year degree. Most trade programs are only two years, granting you an associate's degree in that field, and nearly all of them offer better employment prospects than your average liberal arts degree because they are a "skill." Additionally, because they are a "skill," you are immediately put to work. A friend of mine graduated with a degree in auto mechanics. His first job was not filing or faxing or fetching coffee. He didn't have to "work his way up" to being a mechanic. And there was no ass-kissing or brown-nosing required to ingratiate himself to his bosses so they'd be kind enough to let him finally start wrenching on cars. His skill was too valuable and his employer needed him to do what he was trained to do – work on cars.

The trades also have another benefit in that they're quite barterable. Everybody needs the occasional plumber. Everybody needs the occasional auto mechanic. If you have such a skill, you can barter that skill for something of value, avoiding the taxes on your labor. This "underground economy" aspect of bartering has always existed and is of course illegal. The IRS even requires you list the value of any goods you bartered for so you can pay taxes on it (even though it's nearly impossible to prove barter). But a little bartering here or there isn't going to land you in jail. The benefit in bartering though is that if you are living a minimalist lifestyle and have very little income, a little barter can go a long way. You don't want barter to account for 50% of your income because then you will go to jail, but pulling the occasional gig for a buddy in exchange for six months of haircuts, just makes being independent of the "Education Industry/Corporate America Industrial Complex" that much easier.

Finally, trades are transferable. If you learn to network computers in the United States, you can network computers in Sri Lanka or Singapore or Djibouti. You are not anchored to the US labor market. The world is your employer. You can go wherever the money is, not to mention enjoy the decline by travelling the world.

STEM Degrees

Though not quite as entrepreneurial, you can still pursue a "traditional" career if you major in one thing – STEM. "STEM" stands for "Science, Technology, Engineering and Math" and accounts for degrees like electrical engineering, accounting, neurology, and physics. The reason you can still pull off a traditional career with a STEM degree is that usually these skills are so rare and are in such demand, the power is once again in the hands of the employee, not the employer. For example, say you are a brain surgeon. If your boss even gets the slightest bit lippy, you can walk and be reasonably assured you'll have multiple job offers the next day. Or say you are a petroleum engineer. If your boss degrades you by forcing you to take "diversity training" or "sensitivity training" there's a boss down the road that won't.

Of course, majoring in STEM isn't easy. They are the toughest degrees requiring a lot of math, rigor, and discipline. However, that is what makes them so valuable and why you can command such a high salary. Nearly everybody is capable of earning a STEM degree, but most are too lazy to put forth the effort. Be smart. If you're going to spend the time and money earning a four year degree, make sure it's a STEM degree.

If You Can't Beat 'Em, Join 'Em

My realtor works harder than most people I know. Not only is he a realtor, he is also a contractor, able to build houses from the ground up. After 20 years of working really hard, running his realty business, investing in rental properties, and refurbishing other investment properties, what does he have to show for it?

Not much.

The housing bubble took a devastating toll on not just realtors, but contractors and the overall housing industry as well. My friend, though he worked hard and was very smart, was unable to overcome the economic consequences of the world's worst housing bubble.

But he said something interesting to me one day.

"I'm a teacher."

I said, *"You're a teacher? Did you get your license or something?"*

He said, *"No. I thought I was going to be an entrepreneur. I thought I would work hard, produce value, and create jobs. It dawned on me if I just went to school to become a 'teacher' and worked my pitiful 40 hour work week I'd be way ahead of where I am today."*

Sadly he was right.

Instead of working the 60 hours per week he averaged for the past 20 years, had he just got his education degree at the age of 22, he'd be in infinitely better shape. He wouldn't have had to work anywhere near as much or as hard. He'd have a lot more money in the bank. He'd have better insurance. Not to mention his mental and physical health would probably be better.

However, his observation speaks to something larger. Why try so hard in the private sector when the public sector is so much easier and better-paying? Most public sector jobs are not only easy, they're unnecessary. They are also protected by unions such as the NEA and AFSCME, which not only provide job security, but ensure you're overpaid. Benefits are inexplicably high and you get more holidays than a Scottsdale trophy wife. Forget moral or economic arguments about the usury of the taxpayer or the sustainability of such a system, you cannot afford such arguments. Besides they're moot. The American people have spoken and they believe the public sector is the future of the US economy. So while the government is picking winners and losers in this economy, you might as well join the winning team.

The Military

A final option available for young people is the military. While there are certainly some "health risks" involved, no employer will challenge you or take you as seriously as the military, especially young people. If you want to pursue electronics as a career, not only will they provide the education and training, they'll put you to work on field radios right away. Additionally, you will never find such a generous employer. You get free food, clothing, shelter, health care, and education, not to mention generous pension benefits should you stick it out for 20 years.

It is here the military is a particularly great option for young people. Since nobody else is going to take you seriously until you're 35, you're not missing out on anything if you stick it out for 20 years in the military. In theory you could join when you're 18, have them pay for your college degree, give you training, gain expertise and experience in your field, and when you're 38, BOOM! You retire from the military, collect a pension, and enter a work force that is much more receptive to the idea of hiring you. If I were to do it all over again, this is the route I would have taken.

CHAPTER 7
FINANCE AND INVESTING

"Damn sheeple. Wouldn't know if the Antichrist came up and hit 'em in the face."
-Libertarian Till Death

Whatever you end up doing for a career inevitably the money will start to come in and you'll have to decide how to invest it. If you are pursuing a very minimalistic lifestyle, it may not be a lot of money, but still, some level of financial preparation is needed to enjoy the decline during retirement. Normally this would entail socking away money in some kind of government ordained retirement program like an IRA or a 401k. However, because the financial problems of the United States are so severe the reliability of the entire retirement planning system is in question. This requires we completely rethink saving for retirement, and even resort to non-traditional methods of investing.

Education

While education has already been addressed to quite an extent, it does serve one final role in terms of investing. Specifically, it cannot be taxed or confiscated. Unlike a 401k or your brokerage account, when you invest in an education you are getting the *intangible* benefit of wisdom, knowledge, and skills. Only unless you convert those skills into income via working can those skills then be taxed or confiscated. This makes your education a scalable investment allowing you to make as much or as little as you want, consequently making it impossible for the government to outright confiscate or steal your investment.

One would think given the education bubble and how college is a rip-off, investing in even more education would be foolish. However, it is not the degree or credentials we are going after as much as it is the skills. Thankfully, most of these skills and trades can be self-taught or learned for free online. But there is one instance where going back to the "Education Industrial Complex" and dropping money on a degree might make sense – if you are worried your money might be confiscated. In this case, you have to view your brain as an offshore bank account or "asset protection trust" where you can hide your money away from the government and the parasitic classes. Once you convert that money into knowledge and skills, it's safely locked away forever in your brain, impossible to be taken or stolen. You can then "withdraw" from this account by moving to an environment or country that is not so hostile to production, profit, and success, and simply ply your skills there.

This has been seen before, specifically where doctors and surgeons from Cuba, the former Soviet Bloc and the former Soviet Union defected or escaped communism. Did they lose their houses back in the homeland? No doubt. Did they lose their investments? Of course. But the one thing the government couldn't take away from them was their knowledge. Knowledge that begat them riches when they moved to a free country.

Housing

In general it is advisable you do not purchase a home in the United States. This has nothing to do with the housing bubble or housing prices, but more to do with the fact housing in America is proving to be more of liability than it is an asset.

First, the concept of "homeownership" is an illusion. You don't own your home, you rent it from the county or the state you live in. You rent from the government. Your monthly rent is called "property taxes," but whatever people want to call it, economically it is rent. Since you are renting that means you don't own the asset. Additionally, in a weird economic sense, when you buy a house technically you are buying the right to pay property taxes. Yes, that asset can be used to generate income via a business or renting it out, but in owning the house you also own the life-long liability of paying those property taxes.

Second is the threat of perpetually increasing property taxes. Forever-increasing property taxes undermine the value of homes. Understand any asset, be it a stock, a bond, or a business only has value because those assets generate some kind of profit. Stocks pay dividends. Bonds pay interest. Businesses generate profits. Any time taxes are increased on these profits, the value of the underlying asset goes down. The same economic law applies to property. Property generates rents (or if you live in your home, it saves you rent). So if property taxes go up that lessens the "net rent" or true profit that house generates. With that asset generating lower profits, the value of it goes down.

Third, this is doubly damaging when you consider that your home is likely the single largest asset you own. A very potential scenario (that has already played out in nearly every major inner city) is where millions of people spend 30 years paying off their home, only to have the value of the property be a fraction of what it used to be because property taxes are so high. Bar some kind of constitutional amendment limiting property taxes, you can expect socialism to force taxes to the point homes have no value at all. Either because taxes are too high, thereby undermining the asset, or the taxes drive any would-be buyers out of the market.

Fourth, on a macro-economic level this relationship between profits and value also plays out. America as a country has not generated the economic production necessary to merit the value of its land. Do you want to buy property in North Korea? Do you want to buy property in Cuba? How about the Republic of Chad? Of course you don't. Not only because private property is outlawed, not only because you'd get shot, but because nothing of value is produced in those countries. There is no reason to be there, therefore their land has no value. Not that there isn't value or production in the US today, but that production is likely to decline. And with declining production, you have on a macro-level declining values and asset prices.

Fifth, though not related to asset values, the combination of an over-regulated banking industry and the galactic incompetence of the mortgage industry makes the act of simply purchasing a home a nightmare. Because of the Frank-Dodd Act (among other regulations) banks and lenders must now comply with a crippling level of regulation. This increases not just the costs, but the time it takes to qualify for a mortgage. Making matters worse is the verminously low quality of your average mortgage broker or "professional." Anybody who has filled out an application knows just how many times these morons lose the application, don't get your tax returns, failed to return your call, etc. etc., only to reject your application for one made-up reason or another. And heaven help you if you wish to refinance a house or move, in that you get to go through this ordeal again. In the end the sheer amount of hell you have to go through just to qualify for a mortgage and purchase a home makes homeownership a prohibitive headache.

Sixth, adding to your headache will be maintenance. Most people who rent are completely unaware of the costs in terms of time and money that home maintenance requires. There are small items like painting and carpet, and larger items like replacing the sewer line or re-supporting the foundation. Theoretically these costs are included in your rent, but in being a renter you don't have to spend your time dealing with such issues. Since your goal is to enjoy the decline, eliminating home maintenance from your life forever will definitely help you achieve that goal.

Finally, homeownership is not conducive to a lifestyle of enjoying the decline. Specifically, mobility. In owning a home you are at minimum financially anchored to one geographical location. Yes, you can rent it out, but if that home needs repairs or needs new tenants you invariably have to go back to manage it. Also, you are financially wedded to the local government and its property taxation. Until you sell that house, you have a financial contract you need to abide by or go to jail. About the only instance you should consider owning a home is if you have a family, have a stable career, and cannot fathom living anywhere else. The risks and the headaches are just plain not worth it otherwise.

Traditional Retirement Planning

Traditional retirement planning is based on a simple concept of squirreling away money over the course of your life into various investments, giving those investments time to accumulate and grow, to the point you have enough money saved up so that when you do retire, you have enough money to last you until death. The underlying programs that make up your overall retirement plan fall into three general categories:

1. Government-ordained retirement plans (such as the 401k's, 403b's, 457's, IRA's, SEP's, etc.)
2. Pensions offered by your employer/s and
3. Social security.

With the exception of social security, nearly all these various retirement programs invest in stocks, bonds, and other securities (social security merely invests in government treasuries).   So when you buy some shares of a mutual fund through your IRA, that mutual fund is really just composed of various stocks and bonds. And when your employer socks away some money to fund the company pension, it doesn't just sit there in an account as cash, that money is again invested in stocks and bonds. Again, the idea is that while you work, these underlying stocks and bonds will increase in value providing you enough money to finance your retirement. There's only one problem.

The whole system is flawed.

In creating programs such as the 401k, IRA, 403b, etc., the government effectively "ordained" stocks and bonds as the only or at least "official" retirement investment vehicle. The effect this has had is that people no longer invest in stocks or bonds for what they should (profits), as much as they do for "retirement" or because "they can sell them for more in the future." This disconnect between what gives stocks and bonds their value (cash flow) and the actual price of these securities has resulted in arguably the largest bubble in the history of the US.

With trillions of retirement dollars flooding the stock markets, stock prices have gone up faster than profits. Historically, the average US stock traded at a price roughly 15 times that of its annual earnings (thus the term "*Price to Earnings Ratio*"). However, with all the extra retirement dollars floating around in the market, this has driven prices so high this "P/E ratio" is up to 21.

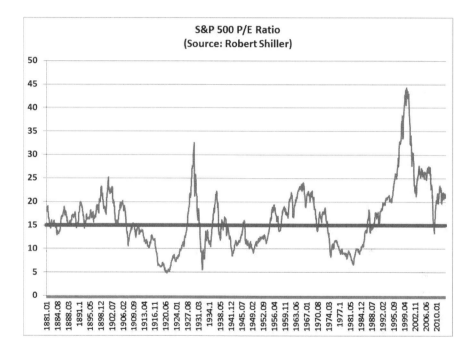

You'll also notice that ever since 401k type plans were introduced in 1978, the stock market has rarely traded at its "normal price level." It has consistently traded higher, at one time nearly 300% its historical average in 1999. And despite two stock market crashes (the Dotcom Crash and the Housing Bubble/Financial Crisis Crash)it still trades at a 29% premium above what its earnings warrant today.

The question then becomes what happens when the Baby Boomers retire and start pulling their money out of the market? Economically, the law of supply and demand dictates prices will come down. And if the P/E ratio is any guide, prices should drop around 30% implying a current day DJIA value of 9,400. This not only makes pensions, 401k's, IRA's and other retirement programs losing propositions, but any investment in the stock market a losing proposition.

Compounding the problem is the lack of economic growth in the United States. Without economic growth corporate profits cannot grow by the amount necessary to rationalize higher stock prices. Additionally, the 2012 election suggests the political environment for corporations will only worsen as public opinion turns against "evil corporations," "evil corporate profits," and "evil corporate greed" (no matter how necessary these things are to their retirement programs). Such souring political and economic climates will not bode well for stock prices in the future.

And finally, if a bubbly market, a politically hostile environment, and a weak economy aren't enough to convince you, then there's always the threat of rescindication and confiscation. Understand the only way the government could get people to invest in the stock market as their primary means of retirement was to give them tax breaks. These manifested themselves in the forms of tax write offs and the absence of capital gains tax in the "Roth" versions of various retirement programs. As the public finances of the United States government become more dire, these tax benefits will be eyed for the chopping block. Rescinding them would not only deny retirees their tax benefits from these programs, but almost immediately result in a dramatic drop in stock prices and consequently the value of your retirement account. Of course, it could even get worse. The government could simply pull an Argentina or a Bolivia and outright confiscate you 401k or IRA. They may even go so far as to confiscate your regular brokerage account, depending on how bad and desperate things become.

About the only arguments *for* investing in traditional retirement plans revolve around two items - "matching" and using them as an inflationary hedge. Since some employers "match" your contributions to your retirement plan, that is free money. Free money that, even if you were to take out of your retirement plan early and pay the penalty, would be money in your pocket and not the coffers of a confiscatory government. Ergo, if your employer is generous enough to match your contributions, it might be worth sticking with a traditional retirement account. As for using your retirement accounts as an inflationary hedge, while it is possible the government would nationalize everybody's retirement plans, it would be near political suicide for any politician to suggest so. Assuming retirement accounts become a third rail of politics and nobody dares to confiscate them, the only option the government would have left to solve its debt problems would be to inflate the currency. This would trigger hyper-inflation, but it would also trigger a jump in stock prices, making your retirement accounts a natural hedge against inflation (for a more detailed economic explanation why this is please read Captain Capitalism post "The Stock Market as a Hedge Against Inflation").

Arguments for and against participating in traditional retirement programs considered, it is impossible to know for sure what the future holds. The economy could come roaring back, profits could increase, government finances could improve and this will all have been proven to be neurotic speculation. However, as it stands right now, it would be wise to diversify at least some of your investments outside the traditional retirement program system.

Non-traditional Retirement Plans

While they may not provide benefits like matching, tax deductions, and an absence of capital gains, non-traditional investments may still prove to be the wiser investment. They are harder to confiscate, they will keep their value during an economic melt-down, they will have higher rates of return than any kind of "Solyndra," and even if an economic doomsday scenario doesn't play out, they at least serve the function of insurance. But before we start listing what kind of investments we're looking at, we have to understand why we would be looking at such investments in the first place.

The primary reason you would be looking to make non-traditional investments is in the case of dire economic times or even economic collapse. If the economy gets really bad or just outright collapses this would trigger several events. First, the value of the dollar would tank as hyper-inflation would be very likely. Second, since there is hyper-inflation, the dollar will also cease being the effective currency, requiring something take its place instead. Third, any investments you have that are electrically stored and recorded will simply be taxed or confiscated away. Fourth, if things get particularly bad you could have a SHTF scenario in which case electricity doesn't work, gas is not supplied, there is no Internet, cell phones don't work, infrastructure collapses, and society no longer works as it did before.

While it is impossible to determine which scenario is likely, or where along the spectrum of economic decline we're likely to be, there are investments that can be made that cover all scenarios. However, these investments all have a couple traits in common.

1. They have intrinsic value, meaning "value unto themselves" i.e.- can be used for something.
2. They are divisible allowing them to be meted out and measured
3. They store well and do not decay, thereby holding their value
4. They would be accepted to have value by most other people. These people may not use these items, but they would realize they have value and maybe even hold onto them themselves.
5. They are physical. They are not stored on account somewhere electronically. You have it in your physical possession.

If you look at that list and remember your high school economics course, you'll start to realize this is nothing more that the qualities and traits of money. And that's precisely what you want to invest in – an alternative form of currency.

The reason why is with any kind of dire economic environment, the currency usually hyper-inflates, wiping out your savings, leaving you with no "effective money" to buy or purchasing things you need in life. So in preparation for such a scenario you want to take the money you have today while it still has value and convert into an alternative form of money that would hold its value well should such a scenario play out. Immediately people's minds go to things like gold and silver, but while those certainly are some of the "traditional non-traditional" investments you might want to make, there are many others that might surprise you.

Gold – Gold is the default backup currency and investment alternative to retirement programs. If you're worried about the economic condition of the United States and the value of the dollar, gold is a logical and common place to invest your money. But while it is recommended everybody have a little bit of gold in their portfolio, because of the recent surge in the price of gold, it is unfortunately priced-out of a lot of people's budgets. Additionally, should a genuine "collapse" occur, gold may become too valuable, rendering even a small amount too precious to part with. It is therefore recommend your investment in gold be primarily in the form of jewelry for a loved one. You'll not only score major points with the lady in your life, but you'll have diversified at least a little bit into the commodities market...just don't tell her it might have to be melted down later.

Silver – Though prices will change, silver is not so expensive that its price precludes it from becoming a default currency. Matter of fact, given its relative value and commonality, it might prove to be an ideal currency in a deteriorating economy. The ideal form you'd like to invest in would be silver dollars or silver bullion. Old US silver dollars (such as the Morgan Dollar or Peace Dollar) have 75% silver in them and can be purchased through coin dealers. If you are just concerned about the silver value and not the collectability of the coins, you can also ask for silver dollar "culls" – coins that are so worn the only value they have is for their silver. Silver bullion (usually in the form of 1 ounce coins) are pure silver and trade at a slightly higher value.

Copper – While copper may not constitute a large part of your non-traditional investment portfolio, you may want to consider it anyway in that it is nearly free. Free in the fact scrap copper can be found nearly everywhere and the US government was kind enough to mint off tons of the stuff in the form of pre-1983 pennies. Even better is while the currency value of those pennies is only 1 cent, the melt value is 2 cents. Though it is illegal to melt US currency, if things get particularly bad, hoarding pennies and later melting them into copper bars may be worth starting a penny collection today.

Guns and Bullets – When you say you're buying guns and bullets people's eyes usually roll over because you're immediate considered one of "*those* people*." Some redneck hick, tucked away in his trailer, fashioning a mullet, eating possum for supper. Stereotypes aside, guns and bullets make great non-traditional investments in that they share those same qualities and traits listed above. If stored properly both will last forever. They're a great hedge against inflation. There is a large and liquid market for guns. And they have the added benefit of being very valuable in case of a SHTF scenario. The trick is to make sure you don't become a "gun nut," never being able to part with any of your guns because they've developed some kind of sentimental value.   Buy them for investment purposes only, knowing full well you won't even fire half of them to maintain their resale value.

Tools – The idea of investing in skills or an education as an intangible investment has already been discussed. But those skills won't mean anything unless you have a quality set of tools to translate those skills into production. Thus, investing in tools can play two roles. One, it will provide a return as you do maintenance and repairs for yourself and others. Two, an extra set of tools will hold its value well and can be sold at a later date if needed. Additionally, while the federal government may confiscate your online brokerage account, it is unlikely they'll come for that extra tool set late at night.

Land – Risks of homeownership aside, owning land can still prove to be a wise investment in a deteriorating or collapsing economic environment. Though it doesn't have all the traits of money, it will hold its value during an inflationary environment and serves a practical function in that you can live off of it. This assumes however the government is protecting property rights and the local government is not taxing it at confiscatory rates. This means owning a plot of land in some far away western state near a water source might be a wise investment.

Spices – If you look at the history of money, you'll see among gold, silver, copper and other things, salt. The reason salt ended up becoming a currency in some cultures is because it has the properties that make it a good money. Everybody needs it, it stores well, it can be measured, etc. However, salt is very common. Not only are there salt mines, you can simply boil away ocean water to get it. But the same cannot be said of all spices. Some spices are rarer than others and that makes them an even better currency-like investment. One only has to look at the spice trade during the 1600's to see how spices serve as a store of value.

Booze – The most-fun currency in the history of the world is booze. It is divisible (you can pour it). It has intrinsic value (ever turn down a drink?). It stores well (ever hear *"Oh no, the vodka has spoiled!"*). And if somebody doesn't want booze, they know someone who does. During the collapse of the Weimar Republic hyperinflation was such that a liter of good cognac effectively became the $100 bill of Germany at that time. And though that was during the 1920's, it is a guarantee booze would still serve in the same capacity today. A crate of booze, unfortunately, takes up more space than say a bar of silver, but thankfully you can drink this currency until you have the appropriate amount in your investment portfolio.

"Survivables" – Things that you need on a daily basis, but store well can also be stocked up. The benefit of these daily items is it is most likely other people need them as well, providing you a liquid market to sell them or trade them at a later date. Aspirin, protein power, over the counter drugs, toothpaste, the items are limitless. However, some things may prove more valuable in times of emergency than merely a decline. Cigarette lighters, even without any gas, have value because the flint and steel can start fires. Antibiotics might prove to have a high value should somebody be in dire need of curing an infection. And iodine pills could prove a profitable investment should anybody start getting thirsty. Again these items verge on the SHTF type of scenario, but are easy enough to pick up on the cheap that it doesn't hurt to have a box-worth of them now.

***

The number of non-traditional items you can invest in or stockpile is literally unlimited. And if you have a keen eye for value and the traits listed above, you can no doubt come up with some of your own. But there is one distinct disadvantage non-traditional investment have and that is you have to physically hold them. This raises several issues when it comes to storage, transportation, and security.

Physical Possession – The main reason you are holding physical gold or physical silver is because you fear it would be confiscated by the government. Yes, you can own a mutual fund that invests in silver or gold. Yes, you can own stock in a copper mining company. The problem is those accounts are no doubt held at a brokerage electronically. All it takes is an act of congress to tax those accounts or confiscate them and there's nothing you can do. Additionally, if things do get bad, it does nothing for you to own "paper silver." You need the actual silver. So if the electricity goes go out and you can't access your online account, good luck redeeming that mutual fund share for a piece of copper redeemable at some copper mind in Australia. This isn't to say having traditional brokerage accounts, or even your 401k plans, invest in commodity based investments is a bad thing (actually, as long as society doesn't collapse completely, such an investment should be considered). It is to say that there is a risk in not personally physically holding *at least some* of these investments.

Storage and Safety – In physically holding these investments you now have to worry about theft. You need to fully think through the ramifications of holding all these things on your person. You need to consider things like security systems, buying a safe or a vault, hiding your valuables, insurance, and not telling anyone about such investments. Guns need vaults. Precious metals need safes. Ammunition shouldn't be stored near the fireplace. And other such things. You may also think about storing these investments across multiple locations in case of fire, tornado, theft or some other emergency to lower your risk of loss.

Transportation – Finally, you have to consider another variable – weight. If you look at gold, silver, guns, bullets, copper, tools and booze they all have one thing in common. They weigh a ton. If you have to move (either because of lifestyle changes or emergency) carrying 2,000 pounds of metal around is going to prove very inconvenient. The weight of these investments may end up proving to be the upper limitation of how much you can invest in them.

***

The "Smith and Wesson" Retirement Plan

Your final option may at first seem very dark and drastic, but it's actually quite liberating when you think it through - simply don't retire. You accept the fact it is unlikely you'll be able to save up for retirement or that the risks of saving for retirement are too great, and you resign yourself to working until you die.

Most people will then ask, *"Well, how will I support myself in my old age if I can't work?"*

Very simple. You drop 33 cents on "The Smith and Wesson Retirement Program." Specifically, you buy a .45 caliber bullet and you take yourself out permanently.

Admittedly, this sounds very extreme and it is very dark, but again, if you thoroughly think it through it is actually very liberating. To understand this retirement plan you have to once again ask yourself what life is all about.

Is it about being in a nursing home, unaware of who you are, where you are, soiling yourself?

Is it about draining the already-inadequate and dwindling financial resources of younger generations just so you can stay alive in such a miserable state for another six months?

Is life about suffering a stroke, losing the use of half your appendages, and being pushed around in a wheelchair until your death?

Or is life about fishing, family, friends, riding motorcycles, hiking, traveling, sailing, drinking, having sex, raising wiener dogs, eating ice cream, and then graciously accepting when it has ended?

The problem in society today is that we put too much emphasis on staying alive instead of living. And if you live in fear of death and try to postpone it a mere couple of months at all costs, you run the risk of ruining all of your life. Saving for retirement is where you run that risk.

In contributing to a retirement program, essentially what you are doing is trading away your youth for old age. The problem in doing so is that when you are older you cannot enjoy life as much as you could when you were young. And since you only get one life, you have to make sure it counts, making such a transaction foolish. Making it worse though is you can really diminish, if not just outright cripple your youth as you try to save for your old age. I know many young 20-somethings who just don't have the disposable income to afford saving for retirement. However, they feel so guilty for not contributing to a retirement program, they end up contributing anyway even though it impoverishes them today.

Can they afford to go the Rocky Mountains? No.
Will they ever see Europe? No.
Can they afford sushi? No.

But hey, at least they got $5,000 saved in that likely-to-be-confiscated Roth IRA!

The Smith and Wesson Retirement Plan avoids all this, relieving you of all the guilt, all the pressures, and all the responsibilities of saving for retirement.

The isn't to say that you won't enjoy life in your old age or that you don't try to live as long as possible. What it is to say is that the majority or at least plurality of your medical and health costs will be incurred in the last six months of your life. Most likely these last six months of your life will not be pleasant. And so if you simply kill yourself when it's clear your condition is terminal or your life is too painful to live, you avoid incurring these costs, meaning you never had to slave away during your youth saving up to pay for them.

The primary contention most people have with euthanasia is a distaste and cowardice of suicide, especially for financial reasons. But people have to be able to discern between suicide and a mercy killing. For example my grandma was diagnosed with Alzheimer's. Over six years we watched her decay in a nursing home from a fully sentient adult into a crumpled up vegetable where the brainstem sadistically kept her body alive. The hell that poor soul must have endured during those six years is unfathomable and makes a 33 cent retirement plan a godly act of mercy.

Finally, if truth be told, the majority of not just the United States, but all western countries' financial problems would go away if The Smith and Wesson Retirement Plan was used. While social pension plans such as social security are commonly cited as the source of the country's financial problems, it is health programs (such as Medicare and Medicaid) that are really bankrupting western countries and enslaving their younger generations. If self-selected euthanasia was commonly practiced, not only would everybody avoid horrible fates such as my grandmother, but our financial problems would literally be solved overnight, rendering this book moot.

CHAPTER 8
PLUNDER

"Since there is no such thing as...the right of the government to seize the property of some men for the unearned benefit of others—the advocates and supporters of the welfare state are morally guilty of robbing their opponents, and the fact that the robbery is legalized makes it morally worse, not better. The victims do not have to add self-inflicted martyrdom to the injury done to them by others; they do not have to let the looters profit doubly, by letting them distribute the money exclusively to the parasites who clamored for it. Whenever the welfare-state laws offer them some small restitution, the victims should take it ..."

-Ayn Rand/"Government Grants and Scholarships"

A large hurdle many Real Americans will face is jettisoning their moral and ethical code when it comes to independence, self-reliance, and hard work. It has been ingrained in us genetically, it has been reinforced socially, and it is part of what we value and pride ourselves on. Unfortunately such honorable ethics are not only obsolete, they are a liability.

With government spending accounting for 40% of GDP and half of all Americans collecting a government check, the rules of the game have fundamentally changed. The social contract between producers and parasites is no longer one of temporary, emergency assistance, needed solely to ensure an economic parasite returns to production as quickly as possible. It is now a political class of slave-masters that purposely, knowingly, and actively vote to live off of the producers. This requires all Real Americans have the courage to acknowledge and accept this fact, as well as change their behaviors accordingly.

Additionally, the debate about being an independent, self-reliant individual is moot. It's not about morality, it's about reality. Most Americans really have no choice. Since government has become so large, it's almost impossible to live an entire life without collecting some form of government assistance. This reality has been forced upon you by a short-sighted and ignorant electorate. But ignorant as they may be, this is a democracy, these simpletons spoke in 2012, and this is the new *reality* you get to live in. You can decide to take advantage of it or be taken advantage of.

Thus, to truly enjoy the decline you must take as much government money as possible. This should prove easy in that if you are living a minimalist lifestyle your income is such that you probably qualify for a whole host of government goodies. But, if you're like me or the rest of all Real Americans, you've never collected a government check in your life. You wouldn't even know where to begin. This requires we find out where to get the government cheese, but more importantly get rid of the guilt when we eat it.

Road Map

The first problem you're going to run into is the fact there is no centralized location to find out which government programs you qualify for. There are three layers of government (state, federal, and local), not to mention charities, each of which you're going to have to approach individually. Additionally, there is no consistency across state and local governments. A program offered in Massachusetts may not be offered in Florida, and a program offered in "Jones County" may not be offered in "Smith County." Thus, to maximize the amount of government money you can get you're going to have to do some leg work and research.

To tackle this labyrinth of government programs, your first step should be to visit with a social worker at the "human services department" or "social services department" at the county you live in. They can inform you what programs you qualify for at the county and are also likely to be informed about different programs offered by the state. They will also be able to direct you to local charities such as food shelves, government housing, soup kitchens, work programs, etc. However, again, there will be significant variance across counties in terms of the programs offered, as well as how knowledgeable your social worker is.

Second, prepare to spend a lot of time on the internet researching different programs offered by your state. While your social worker may be very knowledgeable about the different programs at the county, he or she may not know everything about programs offered at the state. This requires you visit the "human services" web site or the "social services" web site of your state. The quality and organization of these sites will vary state to state, but most states do list the various government assistance programs available to you and how to go about applying for them.

Third, you will want to research the federal programs available to you. Surprisingly, the federal government has actually made this incredibly easy. Unlike local governments, the federal government does have a centralized, "one-stop-shop" website where you can simply plug in your information and it will inform you which programs you qualify for – www.benefits.gov. This web site is not only a great resource for finding out which federal benefits you qualify for, but it also categorizes assistance programs offered by each state. This also makes www.benefits.gov the first web site you should go to when researching state benefits.

Finally, you will want to discover what charities are in town. Most people know where the local thrift store is or even the local homeless shelter. But very few people know where soup kitchens are, or where free meals can be had, or where free vaccinations are being administered. Even though you may not need these services, if you are pursuing a truly minimalistic lifestyle availing yourself of these charities will certainly increase your purchasing power and disposable income. A weekly visit to a church offering free meals will save up enough for a cell phone bill. Getting that vaccination at the local community center saves you the money for the newly released video game you wanted. And picking up free clothes at the local thrift store eliminates $500 in expenses per year. Taking free stuff whenever you can is simply logical and economic.

All of this is, of course, going to take some time. Depending on how streamlined and efficiently managed your local and state programs are, it could take a full month to apply for everything, and that does not even guarantee you'll qualify for assistance. However, you have to consider it like an annuity or finally converting all of your bills to automatic bill pay. Once you put in the work and effort up front it more or less goes on autopilot, yielding time and money in the long run.

Basic Break Down of Government Assistance Programs

If you are a Real American, you are probably only tacitly aware of a handful of "standard" government programs, never having to use them. Though there are an unlimited number of programs across the different levels of government, you should at least be aware of some of the more common ones and how to go about applying for them. They can supplement your income significantly, lower your expenses, and provide you with more free time to enjoy the decline.

***

Federal Programs

Benefits.gov - A quick visit to www.benefits.gov will open your mind as to just how expansive and broad government assistance has become. In the "Benefit Finder" your first step is to select "any benefits that apply" from an appallingly long list. Here is the list:

Career Development Assistance
Child Care/Child Support
Counsel/Counseling
Disability Assistance
Disaster Relief

Education/Training

Energy Assistance

Environmental Sustainability/Conservation

Food/Nutrition

Grants/Scholarships/Fellowships

Healthcare

Housing

Insurance

Living Assistance

Loan/Loan Repayment

Medicaid/Medicare

Social Security

Tax Assistance

Veterans - Active Duty

Volunteer Opportunities

Everything from child care to social security, the federal government has a program to cover you from womb to tomb. Admittedly, the sheer scope and number of benefits the federal government offers is disgusting, but remember, you paid taxes, so you might as well get as much back as you can. Regardless, benefits.gov should be your first stop when researching federal programs.

Food Stamps/SNAP - Though a federal program, foods stamps or the "Supplementary Nutritional Assistance Program," is managed by your state. Thus, in order to qualify for food stamps you have to apply in your state. A central site linking to specific states' application sites can be located here:

http://www.fns.usda.gov/snap/applicant_recipients/apply.htm

The amount you qualify for will vary depending on state, income, age, etc. However you can consult the pre-screening eligibility tool below to see how much you can get in food stamps.

http://www.snap-step1.usda.gov/fns/

Social Security & Medicare (Disability) – Most people when they hear "Medicare" or "Social Security" assume you have to be retired to collect these benefits. Fortunately (or unfortunately) that is not the case. You can claim to be "disabled" and collect a check now.

The government's definition of "disabled" is quite liberal. I had a fully functioning adult come into my dance class one time. She could drive. She could speak. She could learn to tango (which is a difficult dance). But she couldn't work.

Why?

Because she was diagnosed with "bi-polar disorder" and was thus disabled. She was collecting social security at the age of 23.

Another person I know is a fully functional 40 year old woman. She's filed for bankruptcy three times and this is with the subsidy of her parents. Finally cutting her off, she was forced to budget which she failed at miserably. The "stress" of spending within her means was too much to bear, so she quit her job. The wise men and women at the Social Security Administration deemed her "depressed" and she now collects social security.

The point is in order to be considered "disabled" you needn't actually be *disabled.* You just need to be diagnosed with a spurious mental condition and deemed "unable to work." Thus, if you are having a hard time finding a job or just plain don't want to work, consult a therapist, see if you can be diagnosed with bi-polar disorder, depression, or some other such trumped up disability and apply for disability. Besides, it may be the only way you'll ever see a social security check. You can apply for disability here:

Medicaid – Medicaid is a joint health care program between the federal government and the states, once again requiring you apply through your state. The program is designed to provide health care and health care insurance to low income, low asset people. Your hospital bills could be paid directly, or, the state may pay for private health insurance, depending on how the state has set up their Medicaid program. There is no reason to pay for health insurance or health care if it's available for free.

To see if you qualify for Medicaid you can apply here:

http://finder.healthcare.gov/

Section 8/Rental Assistance –Section 8 itself is a program which you apply to belong to. If you qualify, you can then apply for apartments that are certified as "Section 8 Housing" which means you will only pay for a portion of the rent while the government makes up the difference. Like many other federal programs it is administered locally through the county or state, but unfortunately there can be a waiting list in excess of two years.

Since the waiting list may make Section 8 an unviable option, you will have to consider other sources of housing assistance. These sources include low-income housing, government housing, and are primarily handled by state and local governments. To consult what options are available in your state please consult the link below:

http://www.rentassistance.us/

Grants – Not only will the government pay for your food, clothing, shelter, education, and health care, it will also pay you to pursue your hobby as a career or a business. Namely, through grant money. Though there is no guarantee grant money will be available for your particular hobby it doesn't hurt to look. Besides, if you're going to spend hours applying for real jobs (which are bound to be boring, unrewarding, and replete with a commute), then you might as well be applying for grants.

To see if there is any grant money is available for you, check below:

http://www.grants.gov/

Welfare/TANF - "Temporary Assistance to Needy Families" goes by its short name, "welfare." It is cash assistance to unemployed people. It is headed by the federal government, but managed by the states, so benefits will vary. In short you are allowed to have five years of welfare over the course of your life. And after receiving two years of consecutive welfare you are required to find a job. Additional payments can be made, but it will be for the benefit of any dependents you have (though still subsidizing you). Before you leave this planet, make sure to collect for all five years. To start, visit the site below:

http://www.acf.hhs.gov/programs/ofa/help

Head Start/Early Head Start – If finances are tight and you have young children, day care can be expensive. Thankfully, under the guise of "education," "Head Start" and "Early Head Start" will not only baby sit your children for you, but feed them and provide some health services as well. Your child must be "birth to 5 years old" and you need to meet some income requirements. You can consult the link below to see if your children qualify for Head Start/Early Head Start:

http://eclkc.ohs.acf.hhs.gov/hslc/HeadStartOffices

Supplemental Security Income – Though primarily intended for blind, aged, and decrepit people, if your income is low enough you may qualify for this program. Supplemental Security Income (SSI) is a straight up cash assistance program. It doesn't specifically pay for rent, food, or clothing, but assumes your situation is so destitute that's what you would spend the proceeds on. If you are a master of The Art of Minimalism you may meet the income thresholds of this program. To see if you qualify you can apply here:

http://www.ssa.gov/ssi/

WIC – Another federally funded program managed by the states is "WIC" or "Women, infants, and Children." Thought primarily intended for women with infants and children, fathers of children under 5 also qualify. The benefits primarily go to feed your children as well as provide other medical and nutritional support, but the child must be under 5 years of age in order to qualify. To find the WIC office in your state consult the link below:

http://www.fns.usda.gov/wic/howtoapply/

***

State and Local Programs

Because it is impossible to detail all the different programs offered by 50 states as well as all the programs offered by 3,141 counties, it is better to look at services offered by these governments categorically. Most states and counties will have some kind of program falling into all of these groups and should serve to help your financial needs:

Health Care/Insurance – In addition to the federal programs such as Medicare and Medicaid some states offer their own state health insurance program. Like Medicaid these state insurance programs are subsidized or will just outright pay for your healthcare. Additionally while some states may not have actual "health care programs" they may have some form of financial assistance to help you with medical expenses. Visit your local state's health and human services web site to see what programs are offered.

Education/Training – Nearly every state and county has some kind of education or training program. Be it through the public university system, some form of financial aid, or training programs partnered with local trade schools, some subsidized form of education should be available. While it helps to have a non-white ethnicity and two X chromosomes, if your income is low enough you should be able to qualify for some form of government financed training. Your state's department of education should have resources and links that will help.

Cash Assistance – Like the federal government, state and local governments may have programs that go beyond SSI and welfare. Some states are more liberal with the taxpayer's money than others, but again, consult the social services page of your county or state.

Child Care – In addition to WIC and Head Start states and counties may offer their own version of child care and day care. It could be in the form of subsidized day care or a day care vouchers, or conveniently camouflaged as a "school" or a school program ("pre-school," "school lunches," after school programs, etc.). If you do not have the resources to support your own children or you need to work and cannot rear your children, outsource that task to the state.

Housing – Nearly every state, county and major city will have a housing department not only addressing permits and construction codes, but housing assistance. Programs offered can range from subsidized rent to government housing to financing programs used to help keep you in your home. There are also many non-profits that work with the local government to help people with housing. Your local social worker should be able to put you in contact with those organizations.

***

Miscellaneous

While your primary goal in applying for government assistance is to get as much government money as possible, there are other things you can do beyond applying and beyond government programs. Things that will maximize the amount of aid you can get and help you exploit this particular aspect of enjoying the decline further.

Non-profits/Charities – Once you exhaust your governmental options you should turn your attention to non-profits and charities. Though most government assistance programs will no doubt inform you about them, doing your own research can yield the occasional free meal, free clothing, free health care, and subsidized rent. Though the public sector is crowding out charities, charities still do exist and are there to help. Take advantage of them.

Socialist Organizations – Most larger cities have some kind of socialist/Marxist community that specializes in extracting as much money from the government as possible. After you delve into the underworld of non-profits, government assistance, and subsidized rent, you will invariably see fliers and websites for the local chapter or guild of "The Communist Party USA" or some other such organization. Visit their sites or attend one of their meetings. Usually they have a "how to" manual or a "guide" designed for poor people and immigrants as to how to go and collect the most amount of government cheese as possible. It will also be conveniently tailored to your local area.

Move to a Welfare State – Michigan and Minnesota may be welfare states, but they're cold. Why not move to California instead? It's much warmer there and the benefits are even better. Plus, since you're not trying to start a business or be productive, why not head to a state where they welcome spongers? Below is a link to California's Social Services Department so you can get started:

http://www.dss.cahwnet.gov/cdssweb/PG181.htm

"Thanks for the Education!" – Another tactic to consider is having a liberal state pay for your education and training, only to go and work in another state that actually has jobs. For example, you would get the California taxpayers to pay for your certification in welding, only to pack up and head out to the Bakken oil field in North Dakota. Normally, this would upset the Californians, but since according to liberals "education is an investment unto itself," where you actually ply the trade shouldn't matter.

Maneuvering – A lot of these government programs have strings attached in terms of whether you're single, married, living with someone, have dependents, are employed, etc. If this is the case, then switch to whatever is to your own best advantage. For example, if getting married would result in losing the benefit, don't marry, just live with each other. If you need to have a dependent to collect a check, but your ex-spouse has custody of both children, see if you can arrange a deal where you do have custody. If getting a job results in less pay than what the job pays, don't take the job. Whatever the situation calls for, do it.

No Shame – Detesting as this all is, it is the necessary and hardest part of enjoying the decline. Again, you have to remember you are responding to an environment forced on you by other people. It was not your choice. So when you start applying online and walking into the social services department understand there is nothing morally wrong with what you are doing. It will be difficult when you're talking to the social worker, but keep in mind she is only more than happy to hand out government money as that is what keeps her employed. Ideally, once you think through all this - seeing what has happened to our country, seeing what we've become, realizing this is what society voted for - you should have a vengeful glee when you do this.

CHAPTER 9

SHTF

"Fuel generator is great, but in shtf scenario in town it is going to attract whole army. 1000 bic lighters don't take too much space, cheap, you can always trade it for something. "
-Selco/Bosnia 1992

When I tell people about my minimalist lifestyle and how I'm enjoying the decline, I am often asked,

"Well, what if everybody did what you do? What would happen to society?"

I answer them truthfully and dispassionately.

"Society would collapse."

Usually they take umbrage to my obvious indifference.

Regardless, understand there is a risk in that if enough people check out and enjoy the decline there wouldn't be enough producers to keep society going and society could collapse. Also realize that in deciding to enjoy the decline you, on your own microscopic level, are accelerating the decline by minimizing your production. Paradoxically this edges us closer to a situation where enjoying the decline won't be so enjoyable – a SHTF scenario.

Of course, we can't be hypocritical knowingly increasing the chance of a collapse on one hand, while not preparing for it in the other. Therefore, it behooves us to at least acknowledge there is a chance for society to collapse and prepare for that contingency.

Suicide

It is impossible to forecast every scenario or variant of SHTF. It could be short lived, where after a month or so the electricity is turned back on, water flows again, and society goes back to normal. It could be permanent where we revisit the dark ages never to see another Apple product ever again. It could be reformational where the nation no longer exists, but remnant city-states do. Or it could be pure chaos such as a foreign invasion or a civil war. Whatever the case, you can assume a couple of things. There will be no electricity, no cell phones, no medicine, no gas, no internet, no video games, no nothing. If transportation lines are cut, you can expect mass starvation as food is not being transported. If the infrastructure is impaired, disease is likely to break out since medicine is unlikely being administered. It will also be much more dangerous as desperate people will find nothing wrong with killing you if you have something they want. In short, existence is going to be bleak compared to what we're used to today.

The question is whether you would even want to live in such an environment. If the SHTF and it looks like a permanent change with no hope for a better future, then chances are no. Unless you have family, friends, or loved ones you care about, or just a really morbid curiosity to see what subsistence living is like, then suicide would be a very legitimate option. But if you do have a reason to live and it looks like the situation is only temporary, then learning how to survive when the SHTF is vital.

Supplies and Equipment

It does you no good to start preparing for an emergency *after* an emergency hits. You need to prepare now and accumulating the necessary equipment in anticipation for an emergency is the first step.

In a true emergency where you have to leave immediately speed and mobility are your primary concerns. To help expedite your evacuation it is vital you have a "bug out bag." A bug out bag is a large backpack that has everything you need to survive on your own for several days, even weeks in the field. It typically has a metal frame allowing you to carry the most amount of goods. It is waterproof, preventing the contents from spoiling. And each person should have their own bag.

While there is no official list, you will want to have the following items in your bug out bag:

Water and water purifying equipment (iodine pills)
Guns, ammo, and mace/pepper spray
First Aid kit
Identity (passport, driver's license)
Fire starting equipment (matches, flint)
Compass
Flak jacket
Boiling pot (water)
Cell phone/laptop/cords
2 thumb drives of "how to manuals" covering electricity, chemistry, etc.
Maps (with important locations noted)
Camping equipment (sleeping bag, tent, etc.)
Water proof clothing and equipment (plastic tarp, rain coat)
Tools
Sewing kit
Flashlight
Batteries
Physical copy of the US Army's "FM 21-76 Survival Manual."
Seeds
Fuel stabilizer
Cash/Currency (both fiat and commodity money)
Broadcast Radio (hand powered)
2 way radio
Collapsible fishing pole with lures
Non-perishable food
Knife and hatchet
Medicine

Paper, pens, pencil

Understand, however, the bug out bag is the minimum amount of preparation needed for an emergency. It assumes you have to temporarily get away and will either return to your home or find some government shelter. In the cases when you will be in the field for longer periods of time, or you may never return to your home again, stockpiling and preparation must go beyond a simple bug out bag.

In a "long term" SHTF scenario your goal is to resettle in a new location. Since you are essentially "starting over" this means you need to pack as much of your wealth as possible so you have the maximum amount of purchasing power during your trip and when you arrive at your destination. Therefore, these items should be governed by long term thinking, purchasing power, and economics. All fiat currency, all silver, all gold, and any other items mentioned in Chapter 7 that you may have stockpiled should be brought along. If it is not vital you evacuate and move immediately, take the time to bring as much food as possible, even perishable food in that it can be eaten first. Any small personal mementoes, though unnecessary, you may also want to pack to remind you of better times. Also take the time to sit and think about what you need, you may never be coming back.

Procurement

Assuming a particularly dire SHTF scenario, you will inevitably run out of your original supplies and will have to procure new ones. There are varying opinions about this, but you have several options when it comes to getting new supplies.

Ideally, you will have stockpiled enough "currency-like" goods you don't need and were fully intending on bartering anyway. All those Bic® lighters you picked up off the ground while friends mocked you will come in pretty handy when people run out of matches. All those iodine pills you don't need will fetch a pretty penny when you run into somebody suffering from beaver fever. And that extra pistol you didn't need might get you lodging for two months at the local roadhouse. Hopefully, your stockpile of barter-currency will last until society comes back, but if it doesn't you might have to resort to more desperate tactics.

For example, in doing research for this book I called the local drug store and asked the pharmacist what drugs would become most valuable in an economic collapse. I figured a diabetic might pay a premium for a bottle of insulin. However, the pharmacist was quite rude and refused to provide me with such information, which only confirmed I was going to ransack his particular chain of drug stores should the SHTF. Regardless, the point is to find similar such items like life-saving drugs. They are valuable, small, transportable, and in high demand. Yes, you may have to steal them, but in such a dire scenario ownership no longer matters (coincidentally, a nice pharmacist informed me insulin, pain killers, heart medicine, and inhalers are the most valuable).

Another theory of procurement (although cynical) is that you should only carry guns and ammo. In doing so you're aiming to be the most heavily armed person in the area and will simply "take" somebody's water or "take" somebody's shelter. I've even heard on survival discussion boards people bragging, "Thanks for saving up all that water for me!" This approach has its risks in that you'll likely be shot yourself, not to mention for it to be effective you have to be prepared to commit murder. The fact people advocate this, however, is a good reason to carry guns and ammo yourself.

Whatever method or means you use to procure supplies, inevitably the issue will become moot. The reason being is that there are only two outcomes to a SHTF scenario. One, society inevitably comes back online, order is re-established and the production of new supplies relieves you of the task of constantly hunting for existing ones. Or, two, society doesn't come back online, new supplies are never produced, leaving society with only a fixed amount of supplies, which will inevitably dwindle to zero. It is this second case that demands you have a good back up plan.

A Game Plan

Stockpile all the supplies and equipment you want, it won't mean anything unless you have a plan. Where are you going to go? What are you going to do? Who is coming with you? Where are you going to meet? Do you have a network of people? A gang, a group? All these questions have to be answered because a plan of "running around post-apocalyptic America, procuring drugs to hock them for food" isn't feasible in the long run.

Once again, there are two outcomes after a SHTF scenario. Civilization is restored and you return home, or civilization is not restored and you must start anew. Returning home is easy, you simply do it. But starting anew is much more difficult and is why you need a game plan.

Your game plan should revolve around being able to support yourself off the land, independent of the rest of society. This means you have to have not one, but several potential locations picked out in case nuclear fallout, armies, politically hostile environments, etc., logistically negate the others. Different survival specialists may disagree, but the traits of the land you are looking for are
- near a fresh water supply (for drinking and irrigation)
- near a forest (for game, defense, and timber)
- away from any major or medium sized metropolitan center
- in warmer climes where winter is not too harsh

You will need to learn how to farm and hunt, as well as learn how to preserve and stockpile food for winter. You may also want to do some preplanning by buying some land and building a shelter on it today while you still have the use of modern day power tools and infrastructure.

Also key to your plan is the most important thing in life – other people. With society collapsed the only thing you'll have to live for is your family, friends, and loved ones. Without them there really isn't much point in going on. However, in a SHTF scenario people play an additional role – security. There is strength in numbers. This is why settlers didn't head out to the Wild West by themselves or ships sail into German waters during WWII alone. They went in a wagon train or a fleet.

The same principle should be incorporated into your overall game plan. You need to head out with a group of people or a "gang." You should discuss this with your family, discuss this with your friends. You may even want to look around for a local "prepper group" or "survival group" who have a plan to convoy and move out together as a team. An added benefit is not just strength in numbers, but diversification in skills. Following the law of the division of labor, exponentially more work can get done at exponentially higher levels of quality if you have more people. In short, you may have the makings of a highly-functional village that can not only sustain itself, but provide better quality goods and services than some loner snaring rabbits in his far flung cabin.

Leadership

Darwinistically, humans have a genetic, ingrained desire to survive. It is not conscious, nobody really ponders it, it is just the result of millions of years of evolution resulting in the mind wanting to stay alive. Because it is so engrained you don't even think about it twice. If your life is threatened a whole host of automatic biological responses take place in your body, not to mention you're more than ready to kill to ensure your survival. This desire to stay alive is arguably the strongest instinct you have. However, without a purpose in life, this instinct remains just that, an instinct.

Merely keeping the blood flowing and food in the stomach only serves to keep a physiological body alive. You will get the vitamins and nutrients you need for a carbon-based organism to live. But this says nothing about the mind. Without a purpose in life, your mind will start to atrophy and inevitably break. The problem with a SHTF scenario is that it pushes the body to stay alive, but gives your mind nothing to look forward to. Is there a future? No. Is there a purpose to life anymore? Not really. But your body's mindless instinct pushes you to stay alive anyway. It's almost as if the body is torturing the mind saying, "No, we have to keep going," only to have the brain ask, "Why?"

Leadership is what gives your mind a reason and purpose to live.

Leadership provides two things. One, it provides actual leadership, organizing, mustering, and deploying the resources of the team for the benefit of the team. But more importantly, two, it provides the team with a goal, with a purpose:

"We're going to settle on the banks of the Mississippi in Iowa."
"We're going to make it out to Dallas where I hear a new government is forming."
"We're going to make a break for Mexico."

Again, you may like being the Mad Max loner with a morbid curiosity about what subsistence living is like, but most people's minds need more than that. They need a reason to live, and a good leader provides that.

Chances are if you have already prepared for a SHTF scenario and have a game plan you will become a default leader. Most people do not prepare for a SHTF scenario, let alone concoct some sort of plan in anticipation of it, therefore since you at least have a goal, they will gravitate towards you. However, leadership is not for everybody. Loners for example make great leaders, but lack the patience to herd a flock and can move faster and more nimbly on their own. Caretakers can make great leaders, but prefer to deal with the aftermath of tough decisions rather than make them. A leader has to consider everybody, manage them, make tough decisions, and own all of the consequences. If you don't want to lead, then you must throw your lot in with a group that has a good leader with a vision and purpose in life you agree with. You must then do what you can to support that team and its leader.

Basics

As I am not a survival expert, I can only attest to the general economic and philosophical environment you will face in a SHTF scenario and what you can do to adapt to it. What to stock, what to barter, what will have economic value, and (perhaps most importantly) how to find meaning and purpose in life after the SHTF. However, the day to day tasks of surviving (which are beyond the scope of this book) can easily be found on the internet or consulting the US Army's "FM 21-76 Survival Manual."

That being said, an abbreviated version of the basics has kindly been provided by several of my colleagues, which should be supplemented by your own study and research:

Shelter - Though it will depend on your circumstances, shelter is usually the first thing you should address while surviving in the wild. Ideally you'll have a tent, or even better, a vehicle, but if neither are available you'll need to build a shelter with whatever materials are available. Shelter is not just for keeping warm or cold, but also to keep out predators and a place for you to recoup and rest. To build the most effective shelter you'll want to consider using sturdy or grounded items such as cliff walls, caves (if available) and trees as they will not succumb to wind and will provide stability to your shelter. You will also want to consider ventilation. A fire in a cave, no matter how cozy, can burn all the oxygen resulting in carbon monoxide poisoning. An air-tight igloo can have the same effect.

Fire – Fire, whether the temperature warrants it or not, is also vital. It will not just keep you warm, but will also deter predators, fight mosquitoes, allow you to signal for help, and attract other friendly humans. It will also serve your nutritional needs in that you can boil water and cook food.

However, fire can also attract unwanted attention in case you are trying to avoid people. Ideally, you'll have enough fire-starting equipment that starting one isn't an issue, but if you have to start fires by hand it is ideal if you keep a flame going if possible.

Water/Food – With shelter and fire you can start to prepare water and food. Water being your primary concern, you'll need to purify it otherwise there is a high probability you will get sick. There are several purification methods, but boiling water is your best option. Unfortunately, boiling temperature changes with elevation, so just because it's boiling doesn't mean it's hot enough to kill all the bacteria in the water. Other options include treating the water with iodine pills, bringing your own filtration system, or mixing water with small amounts of bleach. Food is simpler in that as long as you're not eating poisonous berries or undercooked meat you should be fine. The primary challenges with food will be capturing prey and preparing it correctly.

First Aid – With no hospitals around it is going to become important you not only have a first aid kit, but you learn how to settle broken bones, make splints, treat wounds, treat infection and even suture wounds. It will also help to know what plants have various medicinal properties in case you run out of your original medical supplies and cannot procure more. Having an instruction manual about first aid with pictures is advisable.

Transportation - In any SHTF scenario it is ideal to have your vehicle for the longest period of time possible. Not only because it will provide ideal shelter and protection, and not only because it can be used to store and transport supplies, but it will allow you to get away from city centers that are sure to have supply, food, infrastructure, disease, and safety issues. Your goal should be to put as much distance between you and any major or medium population center and make it as far as you can to your "safe house."

Unfortunately, in a SHTF scenario it is very likely the refining and transportation of gas will end, meaning it is likely you will run out of gas. So in order to get to your destination (or as far as you possibly can in a vehicle) storing up gas and taking it with you is important. Implied in this is preventing gas from going bad. Gas will usually only stay for about three months and needs some kind of additive to store longer. Usually a bottle of "Stabil" will do the trick, but will only last for six months. Constantly replenishing your supply of gas with fresh gas is key to getting to your final destination.

Caching – Depending on what your "game plan" is, it may require more supplies than you can possibly carry as you make your way to your safe house or final destination. Additionally, if you are ambushed and are carrying all your worldly possessions you will lose everything and have to start from scratch. "Caching" or hiding your valuables at strategic locations helps solve both these problems.

In caching an optimal mix of supplies at pre-selected locations you make your load lighter, your travels faster, and insures you don't lose the majority of your supplies should you be robbed. There are risks of course where somebody might happen upon your hidden cache, you can't find your cache, or your cache is discovered and used as an opportunity to ambush you. But those risks considered, caching some items is still a wise move. Additionally, caching items is an action you can take now instead of waiting for an emergency, and should you never have to use those caches, you now have a treasure hunt for your children to enjoy.

Distill Booze – It's one thing to take as much booze as you can with you. It's another to have the skill to distill it. If you can make your own hooch, you can print your own money.

CHAPTER 10
FIGHT OR FLIGHT

"It's called 'Capital Flight' and it's a feature, not a bug, of socialism."

Dire as things are in the United States and dire as things are likely to become, you do have an option.

You can always leave.

This is what can be considered the "fight or flight" option. Do you stay in the United States and try to fight for a better future or do you leave for greener pastures?

When it comes to staying or leaving there is no correct answer. It all depends on your personal situation and what you want to do with your life. If you have children, a successful career, and a family you love, no doubt it is worth staying in the United States as the most important things in your life are rooted here. But if you're single, a budding entrepreneur, or you have significant earnings potential, fleeing to a freer environment is certainly an option. Regardless of which option you choose there are ramifications and consequences to both. Ramifications and consequences that need to be considered when you determine whether to stay or go.

Fight

If you decide to stay in the United States, understand what you are accepting. You are committing yourself to a life-long fight against the forces and tides of socialism that threaten this country. It will be tiring, it will be depleting, it will consume a material percentage of your life, and it will be never-ending. Minimize yourself as much as you want, make as little money as you can, collect as much government money as possible, no matter what actions you take to enjoy the decline here, you will still have to deal with a progressive and increasing political and social movement taking more and more of your life and freedom. Compounding this problem are the psychological costs in terms of stress and depression you will endure as you watch the country you love continue to be destroyed, despite your best efforts to stop it. The question is not whether you believe this is war worth fighting for. It's whether you believe the war can be won. Sadly, this looks unlikely.

If the 2012 election showed us anything it was just how blindly committed the American electorate is towards fundamentally changing the United States from a country of freedom and individualism to one of mediocre egalitarianism and commune. For a spectacular failure like Barack Obama to get re-elected with such a pathetic message only proves just how delusional the people are and how hopeless the situation is. But there are other factors further cementing this terminal decline. Demographical trends show immigrants accounting for the majority of the increase in the population. However, unlike their 1890's counterparts, modern day immigrants come to the United States not so much for freedom and opportunity, but rather welfare and handouts. Also immigrants, along with the recipient classes of government largess, disproportionately account for a higher percent of births in the country, condemning the country to an even more socialist future. The education system adds further nails to the coffin. Though blatantly abusive, it is thoroughly entrenched, ensuring children are brainwashed to be good little obedient socialists in the future. And if that isn't enough to convince you, the crippling economic realities of the United States' finances should squash any idealistic thinking you may have about the future of the country as well as your future here. In short you run a very large risk in staying here.

However, if there are compelling reasons to stay here, it is imperative you take the appropriate countermeasures to inoculate yourself from the economic and political consequences of the decline. And while we've already discussed such things (minimalism, learning valuable skills, avoiding 401k's, etc.) one thing we haven't discussed is investing overseas.

"Investing overseas" usually takes on the image of foreign bank accounts, laundering money, and shoddy time-share deals. While such things can certainly be considered under the penumbra of "investing overseas," the type of overseas investing we're talking about is having funds or some kind of investment outside the United States. This allows you the benefit of staying here, but provides an insurance policy should you ever need to leave the country.

Investing overseas can take many forms. It can be something as simple as having some money in a foreign bank account. It could be owning a small piece of property in Costa Rica. It could be something more complex such as an "offshore asset protection trust." But whatever it is, it is something everybody should have, regardless of where they live, and will be discussed in greater detail under the "Flight" section of this chapter.

About the only thing you can do in addition to investing overseas is take actions now that will at least help facilitate your moving overseas should you have to at some point in the future. Travel frequently if possible, doing reconnaissance of different countries you're interested in. Become familiar with the people, the culture, the geography, and the economy so you can adapt better. Establish contacts and a network of friends in different countries who are sure to be invaluable when you need to find work, housing, or good conversation. If possible, see if you can obtain dual citizenship in a country of your liking. And finally, use your skills as your passport to different countries. It will be hard getting a work visa as a general laborer, but if you know how to network computers or perform open-heart surgery, immigration and employment should not be much of an issue for you.

***

Flight

Should you decide you have a brighter future outside the United States then you must start making preparations to leave now. However, this is not a light decision to make, and will certainly prove to be the single most important decision you make in your life. If you renounce your US citizenship it is irreversible, meaning you cannot "re-apply" for US citizenship should you change your mind. Additionally, you may not get a visa to visit the United States ever again, making it a distinct possibility you can never visit your homeland or your family every again. You will be turning your back on everything you have known and are comfortable with, and will be throwing yourself into a different culture that will take some significant psychological and cultural adaptation. Thankfully, however, it is not as all black and white as that and there are certain measured and thoughtful actions you can take to ensure you are not making a mistake leaving the country for good.

Research

The first thing you need to do is conduct a ton of research on the countries you think you might be interested in. This means reading everything about them in terms of culture, politics, economics, health, crime, etc. etc. Thankfully, most of the information you need can be found at a handful of resources.

The CIA's World Fact Book is a great place to start. It is the CIA's compendium of every country in the world. It provides a thorough overview of every country in terms of its economy, government, infrastructure, and people. Once you compile the list of potential countries you're initially interested in, I would use the CIA's World Fact Book as a starting point to further whittle the list down.

The Economist's Intelligence Unit is the second place I would go to further conduct my research. The Economist's Intelligence Unit (EIU) is a sister publication of the magazine "The Economist." It is a quarterly review of all the countries in the world and is much more thorough, in-depth, and up to date than the CIA's World Fact Book. Unfortunately, EIU reports are incredibly expensive. Like the CIA they have a "synopsis" page for each country, but its detailed reports that have the most information cost money. Instead of spending the money on these publications I recommend visiting your local library to see if they have a subscription for free. If they don't typically a large city or university library does.

The Organization for Economic Cooperation and Development (OECD) is another great place to go and do more research. The OECD is the single largest resource of economic information in the world. It has reports on every country as well as terabytes of raw economic data. Additionally, they have reports on political and economic issues facing the international community. Tax law, tax harmonization, capital flight, corruption, international trade, etc. You can not only learn about the countries that interest you, but also the political and economic issues affecting the region the country is in.

Transparency International is also a good place to go and visit. Its flagship product is the "Corruption Index" which measures how corrupt different countries are. Its research into corruption, graft, cronyism and nepotism can prove quite insightful and sway you to choose one country over another.

Nationmaster is a great website if you're looking for just raw sociological, political, and economic data. Nearly every variable and statistic about a country and its people can be found there.

There are other resources such as the World Bank or the IMF that have additional research and information about all the countries in the world, but what you will find is that after researching two or three sources you'll run into repeat information. By the time you're done reading the EIU's report, the CIA's report and any research the OECD has you will have consumed the most recent and up to date information available in the world on whichever country you are researching.

Reconnaissance

Reading all the reports in the world about a country will not tell you whether you're actually going to like that country. This requires you actually visit the country and do some reconnaissance. However, this doesn't mean you visit for two weeks, go to all the western resorts, hang out with expats, and do what you would do here, just 3,000 miles away. You need to spend a lot of time living in the country and researching what the real, non-tourist life is like there.

While there is no set amount of time you should visit, I would recommend spending at least a year's worth of cumulative time in any country you are seriously considering. Not only do you get to experience all the seasons and cultural changes that come with it, but more importantly you will discover any "unforeseen deal breakers" which would disqualify that country as a place to live. These "unforeseen deal breakers" are what you really have to look out for because they're "unforeseen." For example, though not outside the United States, when I moved to Wyoming I was very excited because I was finally going to be able to live my dream of mountain climbing and fossil hunting. However, I did not foresee the deal breaker: There is a dearth of interesting or intelligent people in Wyoming. I erroneously assumed people were of average intelligence no matter where you lived. But after having to foreclose on enough trailer homes, watch bloated single moms raid the local WIC office, and wait in line as half of Wyoming still pays by check, I quickly realized a lack of intelligent conversation was a deal breaker. Spend enough time in a country to flush out all the potential unforeseen deal breakers before committing to moving there.

Employment/Business

In addition to finding out what's wrong with the country, while you're reconnoitering you will also want to find out what's right with the country. Specifically, can you make a living in that country? Unless you are moving there with an independently-wealthy amount of money, you'll need to secure some means of employment or income. This will require you get a work visa, the experience of which should tell you how easy it is. If the process is fraught with delays, lost paperwork, bribing officials, this seriously impairs the viability of living in that country. Also if you can't find an employer willing to sponsor you to get a work visa then the ease of which you can obtain one is moot.

However, the goal of moving overseas should not be to simply trade one sucky job here for another sucky job in a warmer climate. It should be to start your own business. Of course most people are intimidated by the prospect of starting their own business, but consider this:

Ever since 1997 I have never had a job that required me to actually show up and physically be there.

Oh sure, the boss required I show up, suffer a commute and spend thousands of dollars every year on gas and parking, but there was no real reason for me to be there. It could all be done over the internet from a home office.

The internet is a game changer in that it has made location irrelevant. It has obsoleted the corporate office and cubicle. It has rendered the billions of square footage in downtown skyscrapers obsolete. It has made commuting unnecessary. It is only because of a bunch of close-minded, short-sighted, aging gray-hairs that people are forced to work at an office. But just because the gray hairs like doing things "the old fashioned way," doesn't mean you have to suffer a similar such fate.

While your ex-boss is waking up at 5AM to get a jump on traffic, you get up at 9AM. While your ex-boss is stuck in traffic, you make some coffee. When your ex-boss is paying for parking, you drag your laptop and lawn chair out. And when your boss sits in his dark, gray office, you lay out on your new office – the beach. Understand that unless you are a tradesman where you physically have to be at work, the majority of work today can be done remotely. IT, accounting, consulting, coding, networking, design, report writing, all of it can be done from a beach. The trick is simply finding enough contract work or your own special business niche to make enough money over the internet to finance your new life overseas.

Network/Contacts

While exploring different countries you should also be creating a network of friends and contacts. This will happen naturally, but you'll want to put further effort into it than merely visiting the local bar. If there are cultural activities, see if you can volunteer or participate. Even if you don't need a job, see if you can apply for one. Play any card games or board games the local old timers do. Certainly contact the local expat group, but see if you can infiltrate and befriend a group of locals. The goal is to have a group of friends that will not only make your life more enjoyable, but should you fall on hard times, you can hopefully find employment.

Dual Citizenship

After spending enough time researching and visiting different countries it will become apparent which country you'll want to live in. This process may take years, but you do not want to rush this decision. However, by this time you will have become familiar with the culture, familiar with its economy, have an idea for a business (or already have a business set up), and be very confident in your decision. The next step is to get citizenship, preferably "dual citizenship."

Depending on the country, you can sometimes have "dual citizenship," meaning you are both an official citizen of the United States and that particular country. Not all countries have this arrangement, but many do. Achieving dual citizenship, however, provides you with a very strategic benefit. You are not committed to renounce your citizenship, but can enjoy the benefits of both countries. It can also buy you time if you're still not sure about your destination country (though if you've applied for citizenship it's pretty much a foregone conclusion). By having dual citizenship it is then simply a matter of renouncing your US citizenship when you are comfortable and ready to commit to your new country.

There is a final added benefit in having dual or even multiple citizenship(s). Since there is no limit on the number of countries you can apply for, you might as well apply for several countries just as a diversification or precautionary measure. This not only addresses the issue you may be denied citizenship in a country, but the application process in some countries can easily take years. Applying for citizenship in multiple countries increases your chances of being granted citizenship, granted it sooner, and with the added bonus of having multiple nationalities.

Bank Accounts/Asset Protection

Whether you're simply scoping out a country or fully intending on moving there, inevitably you will have to set up a bank account. Additionally, you will have to transfer all of your wealth from the United States to your new country. However, if part of the reason you moved was that you feared the United States would confiscate your assets, you need banking services beyond a simple checking account and ATM card. You need asset protection. It is here we have to understand banks, international banking, and some laws.

First, you want asset protection. This means you fear the United States will at some point in the future steal your money. It could be your 401k, your brokerage account, or your bank account. However, the United

States government can only confiscate your money and investments if those investments are held *within US-based banks and brokerages*. If the bank or the brokerage is not in the United States, then the United States government does not have any legal authority to tell the bank to forfeit your money to it. However, it gets a little more interesting.

Say you are a Swiss-based bank, but have a subsidiary in the United States (UBS, Credit Suisse, etc.). The parent corporation does not have to abide by US law, but its subsidiary does. Since the subsidiary is located within the United States the US government can dictate to that specific branch to forfeit your assets. Additionally, the federal government can hold the subsidiary hostage, making demands of the parent company even though the parent company is based in a foreign country. This is why when you're choosing a bank you have to choose carefully.

If your primary concern is that the government is going to steal your money you have to find a bank that has NO subsidiaries or investments in the United States. So say you go to Mexico. And you set up a checking account with a large, international bank based in Hong Kong. You've renounced your citizenship over five years ago. You are not a US citizen. But the federal government, true to your fears, has a shortfall of $2 trillion and has become desperate enough to start confiscating former citizens' accounts. You think your money is safe, but it's not. The US government tells the Hong Kong bank to forfeit the money in your Mexican account, otherwise it will nationalize and shut down the Hong Kong bank's US division. This is what you want to avoid, so make sure the bank you choose has no significant investments or exposure in the United States.

Second, while such outright theft as described above hasn't yet happened, the US federal government has taken a rather bold and audacious action with the implementation of the "Foreign Account Tax Compliance Act" or "FACTA." Of the many things in FACTA is a provision that requires ALL foreign banks, regardless of whether they have subsidiaries here or not, to disclose the balances of all American account holders. Without subsidiaries in the United States and headquarters overseas, you might ask what makes the federal government so arrogant that it thinks it can force foreign banks, that have nothing to do with the United States, comply with this provision?

Well, to enforce it, the IRS will withhold a 30% income tax on any US financial investments. In other words, the foreign banks don't have to have a subsidiary here or even an office here. They just have to own US stock or US treasuries and the federal government will tax those investments should these foreign banks not comply. Forget the added and prohibitive costs this adds to foreign banks, and forget how this scares away foreign investors. Think about what this says about the US government. In threatening a 30% tax on banks outside US jurisdiction on their US-based investments because they won't obey a law that shouldn't apply to them, the government only confirms that your fears of confiscation are not "outlandish" or "conspiratorial," but very well-founded.

Third, do not have any stupid ideas of using offshore banks as a means to avoid paying taxes you already owe. If you made the money while you were a US citizen you will have to pay the taxes on that money. The days of moving overseas to hide from the IRS are gone. The purpose in moving to a lower-tax country is to pay lower taxes on *future* income and wealth, not to escape the IRS. Make your life easier and happier, just pay the taxes.

Finally, you may want to consult foreign banks about what kind of asset protection investments they offer. This can be as simple as a promise they'll keep your information private, to offering safety deposit boxes, to more exotic investments such as asset protection trusts. You may also want to consider consulting with a tax accountant or attorney who specializes in your destination country. A few hundred dollars-worth of investment up front may say hundreds of thousands in the future.

Countries You May Want to Consider

While your research will yield its own results, a basic review of some of the more common destination countries and areas might help initiate your research. There are of course strengths and weaknesses to every country, but these tend to be better than your war-torn Africa countries or terrorist-infested ones.

Caribbean Tax Havens – Sunny beaches, fruity drinks, lots of banks and no income taxes, the stereotypical "tax haven" is pictured in the Caribbean. While all those traits are true, the problem with the tax havens of the Caribbean is a lack of land. And when you literally have trillions of dollars parked on these little islands, property prices tend to be prohibitively expensive. In other words, unless you're already rich, it is unlikely you'll be able to afford living there. Regardless, this is the ideal place to live. Such countries include The Cayman Islands, Bermuda, and the Bahamas.

European Kingdoms and Tax Havens – Though Europe is largely considered socialist, there are little countries, some veritable kingdoms, that are very capitalistic. However, they enjoy GDP per capitas of around $90,000 per person and are reluctant to increase the denominator of that formula. Meaning getting citizenship is only possible by marrying into some of these countries. Such countries include Andorra, Monaco, Isle of Man, Lichtenstein, and Luxembourg.

Stable Western Countries – While the likes of the US, Italy, Spain and Portugal have been frivolous with their spending, resulting in imminent financial crises, other western nations have not been so reckless. Specifically, Scandinavian countries that, though profligate spenders, are also profligate taxers, resulting in little to no national debt. Their economies are strong because of oil and a homogenous population, but will inevitably decline as they follow their socialist doctrine and let anybody into their country, even those who don't care to work or be

Scandinavian. Avail yourself of their generous socialism! Such countries include Norway, Sweden, Finland, and Denmark.

Laid Back Latin American Countries – Though maybe not as nice and polished as their Caribbean tax haven counterparts, a lot of Central and South American countries offer cheaper and more laid back alternatives. You may not be the next international investment banking tycoon, but you can relax, enjoy a cheaper cost of living, and be given your privacy. Typically the destination for retiring expats, these countries include Mexico, Costa Rica, Belize, and Chile.

Strong Asian Countries – Asia has the benefit of strong economic growth, traditional, cultural values, a hard work ethic, and a desire to pursue STEM over the liberal arts. Their growth rates have trumped their western counterparts, giving people the opportunity to pursue careers if they so desire. Though not "tax havens" where you'd loaf around, they do have lower taxes than the United States and better work opportunities if you're willing to learn the language. Countries include Singapore, South Korea, Hong Kong, and Thailand.

Australia/New Zealand – Though not tax havens, Australia and New Zealand do have better finances than the United States. Whereas the average American is now born with $200,000 in debt the average New Zealander or Aussie is born with just a tenth of that. Their economies are also stronger because of commodities and mining. You also have the benefit of them being modern western nations will all of the features, as well as the fact they speak English.

***

Regardless of which country you inevitably choose, realize it is going to take a significant amount of effort and time to make a wise decision. You need to research every aspect of the country, you need to live in the country, and you need to make sure it is a better option for you than the United States. Additionally, you must go well beyond the basics covered here. Reading about expatriating, finding discussion boards, becoming fully aware of the ramifications of renouncing your US citizenship, and consulting tax accountants should all be part of your homework before moving overseas.

Resources

To help further supplement your research, please consider the following links below:

http://escapeartist.com/
http://americansabroad.org/
https://www.cia.gov/library/publications/the-world-factbook/
http://www.oecd.org/
http://transparency.org/
http://www.nationmaster.com/index.php
http://www.expat-chronicles.com/
http://englishteacherx.blogspot.com/
http://www.eiu.com

CHAPTER 11
REVENGE

"You ignorant, servile scum!"
-David Webster

If a group of people came in and destroyed your country, destroyed your family, destroyed your life, and stole your future, your natural, mentally healthy reaction would be simple – revenge. You would hunt those people down and kill them. Unfortunately it wasn't some roving band of post-apocalyptic bandits that did this to you, it was the electorate of the United States. And unfortunately this electorate did it legally under a democracy.

Since this is a democracy, no matter how much damage the electorate causes, you have no recourse. It doesn't matter that it's unlikely you'll ever have a successful career, it doesn't matter that it's nearly impossible to start a family, it doesn't matter you have no future. By living in a democracy you agree to accept majority rule for better or worse. Ideally this rule would be "better." The electorate figures things out, puts 2 and 2 together, and inevitably comes to the logical conclusion a minimal state and maximum freedom is the ideal form of government. But as evidenced recently, the electorate is impaired, it's ignorant, it's naïve, and it's brainwashed. Consequently, the people not only get the government they deserve, the minority gets to unjustly suffer the consequences.

But what makes things particularly frustrating for the minority is one of forced-inaction. Because this is a democracy any form of revenge or retaliation would be considered tyrannical or dictatorial. The people have spoken, the majority got its way, opposing this would be hypocritically forcing the minority's view on the majority. Sadly this leaves Real Americans with no option but to sit and take it. It also makes most of us feel helpless. There's no way to strike back, there's no way to circumvent the consequences, there's no way to turn the boat around. There's nothing we can do but futilely write letters to the editor or start blogs. It is an issue of losing control over our futures and our lives, and there's nothing we can do to avenge ourselves, let alone receive an ounce of recompense or justice.

However, things are not as hopeless as they first might seem. There are legal measures you can take to exact your toll of revenge. There are things you can do that will ensure your life is better than others. And as it just so happens there are much more powerful forces at play that will deliver such a devastating blow of revenge against the people who destroyed the United States, that you could only dream of delivering such a blow. The trick is to open your eyes to see it and savor it when it happens.

Fun

In the summer of 2011 I was fortunate enough to enjoy a two month vacation in the Black Hills. I climbed every sizeable peak in the mountain range, enjoyed nearly all their trails, managed a 16 mile hike through Badlands National Park, chased tornadoes, hunted the elusive "fairburn agate," and put well over 1,000 miles on my motorcycle. I was living a dream very few people ever have.

Since I was an avid hiker I hooked up with the local hiking group and met a girl who would become one of my best friends – Amy. Amy was a doctoral candidate in psychology interning at the local hospital and was one of the few people I've met who could keep up with me hiking. Naturally, since she could keep up, we spent hours in the middle of the Black Hills availing ourselves of some of the most beautiful scenery in the world. But of the literally scores of hours of conversation we had the most interesting thing she said to me was,

"You know, I was hiking in Rocky Mountain National Park and I saw the

first black family I've ever seen in any national park. It was nice to see African Americans enjoying a national park."

I had noticed this before. There was definitely a dearth of black people at national parks. Matter of fact, I couldn't remember seeing *any* black people at any national park and I had been to many. I chalked this up to the fact most national parks are in states where there is a low black population. But I also knew the relative poverty of blacks also deprived them of the disposable income necessary to visit national parks.

We discussed why we thought this was. Amy had worked with an inner city youth group at a local charity as part of her doctoral program (the majority of the group being black). She pointed out not just the lack of disposable income, but that the primary concern of these kids was finding employment, finding housing, and just getting their lives together. Which national park they were going to visit next never crossed their minds. They didn't have the luxury.

However, there was one luxury they did have. The luxury of receiving more government money than I've ever received. Housing, food, health care, etc. Not to mention they got to go to a free baseball game on the charity's dime. But that was the interesting observation. How was it Amy and I, two relatively poor people who never received a dime in government money, were out in the Black Hills enjoying all of its beauty, while these poor kids, who had the benefit of government money, were just trying to put their lives together?

The answer was simple.

The majority of government money wasn't going to enrich them so they could afford trips out the national parks, but to compensate them and shield them from the full costs of their mistakes or the mistakes of others.

Understand these kids weren't "nice little kids who just happened upon bad luck," but kids who already had track records, ran into trouble with the law, and were now young adults incapable of adapting and surviving in society. Whether this was because they consciously committed a crime or they had poor parents, it doesn't matter. A mistake was made, costs were incurred, and government money went in to pay for it.

Now I bring up the lack of black people in national parks is not for racial reasons, but for statistical ones. Specifically, to form a control group. No group of people (along ethnic, religious, gender or any other lines) vote for socialism more than blacks. Additionally because of poverty, out of wedlock births, crime and so forth, no group of people suffers a lower standard of living in the United States than blacks (though some Indian reservations do have lower standards of living). Because of this blacks also receive a disproportionately high amount of government subsidy. But do you see any of them at national parks?

Sadly no.

The larger point is not to mock or ridicule blacks, but to use them as a control group to point out one very important thing for all races. Despite trillions in income and wealth transfers, recipients of government largess (regardless of race) still don't have the disposable income to enjoy life. The vast majority of government checks are cut not to make somebody richer than you, but to negate the costs of their mistakes. To merely bring them up to par. To keep them above the poverty line.

The revenge we should take from this is the majority of people who forced socialism on us have such sad lives that even with government subsidy they still will never enjoy the lives we do. The single mom of four may get free baby formula on our dime, but she will never climb Harney's Peak. She will never see Mount Rushmore. She will never see Paris. "Jessup the Red Neck Meth-Head" may be collecting welfare, but he'll never enjoy a good jazz club, an exquisite Gibson, or a finely-tailored suit. The parasites of society are parasites because they made crippling mistakes that will forever ruin their lives no matter how much government money is thrown at them. And even though they may get free health care, free formula, and free tuition, they will never live the happy, successful, and fun life you will.

Happiness

All of this, however, hinges on one simple, but important thing. In order to exact your revenge you need to actually go out and have fun. You need to go out and enjoy your life. You need to be happy.

Merely moping about, lying around, lamenting the loss of the United States to the point it cripples you will avenge no one and nothing. Worse still is living in fear of the economic collapse of the country, scaling down your spending, being unnecessarily frugal, as if you are somehow personally responsible for its trillion dollar excesses. This only prevents you from enjoying life today for a future that will be confiscated tomorrow. You must go and have as much fun as possible in life starting right now.

Unfortunately, it isn't like you can throw on a switch and "POOF!" you're having fun, being happy. Additionally, you don't want to fake it being "faux happy" as if you're on anti-depressants. You want to be genuinely happy. But having fun and being genuinely happy actually takes a lot of work. And given the political and economic environment recently, most Real Americans have an uphill battle.

First, to revisit Chapter 1, you need to acknowledge and realize what you do and do not control. The single largest source of frustration and grief comes from people trying to change what they cannot. In learning this very important lesson you achieve a necessary and first step towards becoming a happier person. Again, I would be lying if I said I never let things outside of my control bother me, but it is necessary to at least try.

Second, actually go and do fun things. In doing fun things you will naturally become a happier person. However, it is not so much that people don't *want* to do fun things as much as it is people *allowing* themselves to do fun things. Either it's not in the budget or you don't have time or you just can't get yourself to click the "buy" button when booking a flight. You have to train yourself to stop coming up with excuses, commit yourself to doing fun things, and pull the trigger.

Third, do grandiose-fun things. The two month vacation I took in the Black Hills was the third of three, and it won't be the last. The two week, 2,000 mile motorcycle ride I took this summer was a spur of the moment deal where after putting in my two weeks' notice I was informed they would pay me for those two weeks, but I wouldn't have to show up to work. 10 minutes later I was on my bike.   And this spring, weather permitting, I intend on chasing tornadoes for a full month. Saner people may want to visit Europe or go on a world tour, but whatever it is, do something big and grand that you've always wanted to do. Want to bike around Italy for a summer? Quit your job and do it. Want to visit the South Pole? Cash out your 401k and do it. Yes there is a risk you may not have a job when you come back, but that's better than living a life where your biggest achievement was a "successful career" and "never seeing the South Pole" a regret.

Fourth, work less. Work is the opposite of fun. It's like matter and anti-matter. If work and fun ever came in contact you'd have an explosion. You need to minimize work in your life, putting it where it belongs – dead last on your priority list. Ideally you could be one of the lucky few who actually enjoys their job, but if you're like everybody else realize when you're working that is time that could be spent having fun.

Finally, since being happy and enjoying life is so important, I strongly recommend reading Dennis Prager's book "Happiness is a Serious Problem." It delves into the topic of happiness more thoroughly than we do here and makes a much more compelling case to be happy.

Ultimately achieving happiness is not something that will happen overnight. Most people will have to completely rethink their life, refocus their lives from work to fun, and put great effort into adjusting their attitude and psychology. But if there is a compelling reason to achieve this epiphany it is not so much revenge or living a happier life than other people, but avoiding the misery an unhappy life brings. Of course you can't "choose" to be happy all the time, but you can make efforts and strides to be as happy as possible for as much of your life as possible, thereby minimizing misery. In living such a life you will have your revenge.

Better People, Better Lives

The benefits of having higher-quality people in your life are obvious. If you have intelligent friends, you will have better conversation. If you have interesting and eclectic colleagues you will have a more interesting career. If you have a hotter spouse you will have a better sex life. And if you have a stronger character you will have a better family. In general the higher quality of people in your life, the higher quality life you will lead. But the added benefit of having good people in your life is that it strikes at the biggest weakness of leftists –envy.

Understand at the core of leftist ideology is the concept of equality. We can see this in the left's demand to constantly redistribute more and more income, and there is no doubt in anybody's mind that deep down inside most leftists would love nothing more than to achieve 100% equal income distribution. However, the left's desire to make things "fair" doesn't stop with income and wealth. There are other instances of inequality in life. Intelligence, prestige, skill, looks, strength, talent, etc. Even things that do not speak to a person's character or intelligence is deemed "unequal" such as height or race or sex. And if you go beyond the left's fiscal ideology and look at its social ideology, you can see they are actively attempting to make things equal in these non-financial aspects as well. "Fat acceptance," not keeping score at little league games, the elimination of "he" and "she" in the Swedish language, etc. In short, they wish to eliminate ALL differences between ALL people.

The problem in doing so is that you eliminate the individual. And individuality is what makes humans the most cherished things on Earth. The reason leftists pursue the elimination of individuality, however, is because they're afraid of being inferior. Sadly, all they manage to achieve in surrounding themselves with boring, equally mediocre, like-minded people is a boring, equally mediocre life.

It is only logical, then, what we can do to get our revenge from these people. Rub their faces in it.

Understand in surrounding yourself with unique, eclectic, high-quality people your life will be superior to theirs. While you're all laughing it up at the local cocktail party listening to some Dave Brubeck, Jebediah and Peggy Sue will be drinking swill listening to some painful country song in their double-wide trailer. While you're looking at real art and appreciating masters like Monet and Rembrandt, the faux-intellectual liberal crowd will be suffering at the latest minimalist art opening of some talentless trust fund baby. While you're walking down the street with your hot-bodied girlfriend as she dons 6 inch heels, Tanner the Effeminate Liberal Male will look at his eco-warrior, portly, vegan girlfriend and contemplate suicide. And while your masculine husband gives you such a mind-blowing orgasm you start to flirt with unconsciousness, there's a feminist somewhere just trying to have one, but she can't because she can't fully imagine Tanner is George Clooney.

The left has to surround itself with mediocre, hypocritical, compliant bores in an attempt to protect their egos. Remind them of that fact every day by having superior friends and living a superior life.

Enjoy the Best of American Culture

It was 1994 and I had purchased Victor Borge tickets six months in advance so I could get the best seats in the house. Since I had six months I figured it would be no problem finding a date. But after asking out the first three girls or so, I realized I had an unforeseen problem.

None of these girls knew who Victor Borge was.

This then required my 19 year old self to try to explain who he was, what he did, and why they should give up their Saturday night and spend it with me. This extra explanation made it a poor sales pitch and I ended up having to take one of my female friends, not the yet-to-be-discovered femme fatale love interest I had in my imagination.

I was fortunate enough to see Victor Borge once more in 1999 before he passed away, but my difficulties in landing a date back in 1994 for something that I thought would have been a slam dunk taught me an important lesson. Most women my age lacked any culture.

When Casablanca was being shown at the local student union, it was only the old professors who showed up to watch it. When a great jazz band was playing, I could only find my friend Dave to attend. And have you ever tried to woo a girl into your dorm room with the offer of watching "Hogan's Heroes?" If it wasn't tickets to see the latest, lamest, goofy-named band of the 90's the girls were just not interested.

But what I couldn't figure out was how couldn't they be interested? How couldn't you want to see Casablanca? How couldn't you want to see Victor Borge? And how could you go through life without watching Hogan's Heroes? They had no idea what they were missing out on, and also had no idea just how sad and pathetic their lame-ass "grunge" culture was by comparison.

Of course the lack of culture is not relegated to women, and it certainly isn't relegated to the 90's. The sad truth is today nearly everybody of all ages and both sexes are woefully uncultured and uninformed about the greatest cultural accomplishments of America. Part of this is simply the debasement of American culture and media producers playing to the lowest common denominator. But also driving this unappreciation for American culture and classics is a smear campaign by the left.

Though not consciously overt, there is a drive or a desire, largely driven by cultural leftists, to replace what is considered "good" or "quality" with anything that is "new" or "different." To replace what is considered "traditional American culture" with "post-modernism." Or to put it more bluntly, to replace excellence with crap. The reason for this is laziness. Since leftists can never achieve the accomplishments and successes of their predecessors (or better put, they *choose* not to) they attempt to redefine what is "quality" and what is "excellence." And thus you get cultural decay.

This cultural decay can be seen in nearly every aspect of American cultural life. Instead of Victor Borge, you now get Margaret Cho. Instead of Louis Armstrong, you now get Snoop Dog. Instead of Peter Gunn, you now get Sex in the City. And instead of Kelly's Heroes, you get "Farewell, My Queen." However, it is here you will get your revenge.

Understand leftists' allegiance is first and foremost to their ideology, not themselves. Since the individual leftist typically produces nothing of value and therefore has no value as a human, they must derive their value through their ideology. This condemns them to forfeit their individuality and commit themselves to leftism like a religion. Consequently, it also forces them to accept the tenets and principles of the ideology over themselves. However, the tenets and principles of leftism are primarily that of mediocrity and commune, not excellence and individualism. And without excellence and individualism, you cannot have great achievements in culture. Thus, not only is the leftist forced to forfeit their individuality and live a lie, they are forced to "enjoy" an inferior cultural life.

For example, deep down inside every liberal wishes they could drive a Ford Cobra Mustang, but they can't. Their ideology mandates they drive the Prius. Deep down inside they wish they could afford that McMansion, but they can't. Their ideology mandates they live in some crummy "diverse" neighborhood. They would like to look at real works of art, but post-modernism mandates they faux-fawn over the latest minimalist garbage. And while they would love nothing more than to watch "The Expendables," their ideology commands they applaud the latest boring Indie film.

The result is what we can all visually see. The sad, never-smiling leftists. The "vegan-parents" who send their poor kids to "drum circle camp" instead of "corporatist" Disney World. The ugly hipsters trying their best not to conform, only to become the epitome of conformity. The worthless liberal arts doctorate who can't find a job, but sublimates it through bragging about her green credentials. All the while keeping up an air of condescension when it comes to rubes, you hicks, who couldn't possibly have the intellect to understand the finer and deeper points of their obviously-superior culture.

But don't be fooled for a second.

They are hollow and they are unaccomplished. They will never get to view the classics. They will never permit themselves to enjoy the best American culture has to offer. And if they do, they will have to force themselves to mock it, ridicule it, and deconstruct it simply to validate their inferior culture. So while you're watching The Dean Martin Show or taking in some 1940's architecture, know they're watching the latest NPR documentary or banging away in a drum circle, hating every second of it.

***

Schadenfreude

The "Reality Principle" is not the Freudian principle found in psychology, but one I made up to explain a phenomenon I was witnessing in the real world. Simply stated, if you base your decisions in reality, they will be more effective. Most people would think this is common sense. *"What fool would not base their decisions in reality?"* However, humans are interesting creatures. And though basing your decisions in reality would seem a given, when you introduce politics, ideology, and religion into the mix humans don't think so clearly.

The main reason is that an ideology, whether political or religious, tells people they can have their cake and eat it too. This isn't a slam on all religions or political parties, but rather to point out that most ideologies tend to lie to their followers about the realities of the world. And if people are intellectually weak or intellectually dishonest enough, they will violate the Reality Principle and allow themselves to believe it. Unfortunately there are some consequences to ignoring the Reality Principle.

Take for example three groups of people that are considered leftist or anti-American:

Blacks who vote democrat
Feminists
Radical Muslims

All three follow a religion or ideology. All three ideologies are erroneous and flawed. And all three groups suffer consequences.

Democrat Blacks

Blacks who vote democrat do so because they believe government intervention is the solution to their problems. Lied to by race pimps like

Al Sharpton, they believe their problems are solely caused by discrimination and believe the only solution is to redistribute non-black income to compensate them. The reality, however, is that their situation is largely self-inflicted: 70% of children born out of wed-lock, inexcusable parenting, an acute case of "Woeismeism," etc.

The problem is that the reality does not jibe with the religion they believe in. Additionally, the political arena has been so manipulated and controlled, nobody can speak candidly and truthfully about the cause of black poverty. Therefore, the same tired policies are tried and tried again to no avail because those policies, though politically correct, do not address the real cause of black poverty. They do not adhere to the Reality Principle.

What are consequences?

Unfortunately, what you would expect when decisions aren't based in reality - continued black poverty. Despite the stated "intention" of leftist ideology, blacks still suffer an effective second class citizenship. They have lower incomes, lower educational attainment, lower life expectancies. Absolutely no progress has been made pursuing the democrat's socialist policies. You would think over time democrat blacks would realize this and switch parties, but here is another sad realization. They value their political ideology more than themselves.

If there is proof that democrat blacks love their ideology more than themselves one only has to look at Detroit. Detroit is the epitome of the democrat black's ideology. Government money, government intervention, government regulation. Never mind Detroit is a cesspool. Never mind Detroit offers nothing to no one. Never mind the damage democrat and socialist policies forced on its primarily black citizenry. It is a death pact between democrat blacks and socialism.

The results are actually quite sad. Because their commitment to their ideology is so strong, democrat blacks condemn themselves to a life of second class citizenry regardless of the promises of their ideology. Worse still is they have blindly enslaved themselves to the political leaders of their ideology – the democrat party – making them nothing more than tools for their political masters. The victims are not so much the people who have to pay additional taxes to subsidize the likes of Detroit and its citizenry, as much as the people who blindly accept such a sad existence.

Feminists

Feminists are even more delusional than their democrat black counterparts. At least democrat blacks adhere to human nature in that redistributing income benefits them. Feminists go against human nature.

Of the many flawed principles of feminism, the largest one is that men and women are the exact same. Not just equal, but the *exact same*. Specifically, feminism believes that "gender" is not a physical concept, but rather a social concept. Meaning if you were born male, you really aren't male. Society programs and conditions you to be male. Your genitalia doesn't matter. Ignore millions of years of evolution. Ignore nature presenting you physical evidence in different genitalia. Ignore the preponderance of evidence in the animal kingdom. Nope, males and females are the EXACT SAME.

From this they not only extrapolate erroneous philosophies about the sexes, but make irrational demands of society. Again, why you have the Swedes banning "him" and "her" from their language, why some parents are bringing their children up "genderless," and why feminists demand female firefighters and military combatants (despite their physical incapabilities). But what is sad is how such an outlandish and idiotic philosophy could even gain traction in the real world. It is once again a testament to the intellectual weakness and intellectual dishonesty of people who would subscribe to this.

The question is what are the consequences for ignoring the Reality Principle and believing in such poppycock?

Obviously children brought up "genderless" are guaranteed to have problems, getting the crap kicked out of them on the playground being their immediate concern. There are safety concerns about professions where physical strength is mandatory, and thus safety is compromised when we put affirmative action over people's lives. Traditional and specialized male and female roles that served to benefit the household and society are eliminated. But if there is a true cost to modern day feminism it's that it corrupts the most important thing in men's and women's lives – namely, women and men.

In denying the differences between men and women, all feminism has managed to do was take away all the fun. Unless you are gay, most people like the difference! Men like women, and women like men. Men like long legs, big boobs, tight butts, and long hair. Women like big muscles, chiseled facial features, brute strength, and stubble. And if you look at men and women physiologically they were made for each other. What evil would want to take away these differences and the corresponding fun, I don't know. But while men certainly suffer a lower-grade of woman due to feminism, it is women who actually pay the higher price.

In ignoring the obvious and glaring differences between the sexes, feminism started dispensing erroneous advice to women. Worse, since it was primarily women who purported the theory about there being no such thing as "gender" in the first place, it was only a foregone conclusion the advice they would dispense would be "female-centric." This biased approach completely ignored men and male sexuality and did nothing to incorporate them into their new "model" of how the sexes should work. The resulting advice was not only completely ineffectual, it was outright damaging.

Despite biological hardwiring, women were told they don't need men and don't need marriage. Despite biological hardwiring they were told they needed to be the leader. Despite biological hardwiring they were told "beauty" and "femininity" were oppression. And despite biological hardwiring they were told rearing children was demeaning. Divorce sky rocketed, families fell apart, and government spending required to deal with the social consequences skyrocketed.

But probably the single worst thing feminism has done to women was lying to them about what men *should want*, and not focusing on what they *do want*. And in doing so torpedoed any believer's chances of finding a man and getting married. Today millions of women in their 20's, 30's, and 40's have such corrupted thinking about dating, men, courtship, and marriage no man in their right mind would propose to them. This is evidenced in statistical trends showing a higher and higher percentage of women never getting married:

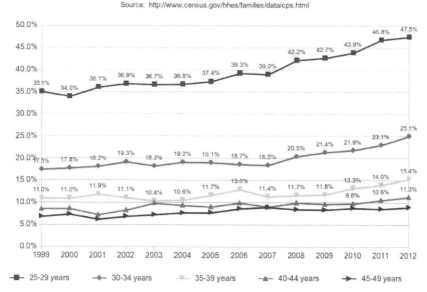

Percent of US White Non-Hispanic Women Never Married by Year and Age, 25-49

Source: http://www.census.gov/hhes/families/data/cps.html

http://dalrock.wordpress.com/

Naturally feminists will retort they don't need a man, they don't need to get married, fish-bicycle, etc. However, ask yourself the question – have you ever seen a happy feminist? Of course you haven't. The constant scowl on their faces, the empty look in their eyes, their bitter thin lips tells you no matter what they told themselves, there are differences between men and women and they will never get to enjoy them. They are the most miserable women on the face of the Earth. And if other women are foolish enough to deny the Reality Principle and swallow this feminist claptrap whole, they too can expect to be equally miserable.

Radical Muslims

Though not political, practitioners of radical Islam have the same traits as feminists and democrat blacks. They value a religion more than they do themselves and suffer miserably for it.

If you think about it, the end game of radical Islam is quite sad because if it were ever to come to fruition, it would immediately collapse. Let's just say radical Islam takes over the world.

Who are they going to blame then for their failures?

If you look at radical Islam there is always an "enemy," always a "boogey man" that they can point to and blame for keeping them down. If it isn't Israel, then it is the United States. If it's not the United States, then it's the West. And if it wasn't the West, then it would be something else to the point that if radical Islam dominated the world, they would have to start blaming aliens as to why things aren't going their way.

Like most religions or ideologies, radical Islam is inherently flawed. The cause of its problems are internal and self-inflicted. When you train people to hate other people simply because they don't believe what you want them to, your problem isn't the world, it's you. And subjugate the entire globe, you're problems will not go away until you do.

Again, what kind of lives do radical Muslims live? What is their life like because they refuse to adhere to the Reality Principle?

Like feminists, have you ever seen a happy, smiling radical Muslim? Do you see them enjoying life and making the best of it? Of course not. The vast majority of times you see radical Muslims they're angry, they're pissed off, they're burning some flag, and they're shooting guns into the air. The only time you do see them when they're happy is when they've managed to kill a score or more of infidels...only to immediately get re-angry at their never-improving situation in the world.

The consequences are again sad and miserable lives. There is no happiness. There is no joy. It's so far away from reality that many of them come to the conclusion their best option is to kill themselves.

Delusion

The reason for bringing up the three aforementioned groups is not to pick on feminists, liberal blacks, or radical Muslims, but to highlight a pattern or commonality between all three. They're delusional. Their ideology is not based in the real world, their decisions are not based in reality, and they suffer miserable lives for it. But being delusional is not relegated to just these groups. Any group that doesn't adhere to reality is delusional. And the single largest group of deluded people are leftists and socialists.

Such a broad claim will naturally be debated, but at some level every leftist and socialist is delusional, if not for any other reason than socialism, like all ideologies and religions, is inherently flawed. It's key flaw being it puts the government before the people. Understand this is a critical flaw because the government and the private sector have a "chicken or the egg" sort of relationship – which one came first?

Did the government form and then people start to rally around it, starting an economy and forming a society?

Or was a society and economy already forming, growing to the point it needed a government to govern that society.

The answer is not only obvious, *it's spelled out in the word **govern**ment* - implying something needed to already exist in order to be governed.

This simple fact should be the foundation for any form of government. The government is for the people, not the other way around. For if there were no people, then there would be no need for government. Yes, through fanciful financing, class warfare, and Keynesian voodoo we can delude ourselves that government has some kind of inherent value, but in the long run, unless the people and society are put first, that society will collapse.

The larger point is not to debate the merits of Keynesian economics or how governments form, but to highlight that on a fundamental, basic level any ideology or religion based in socialism is inherently flawed and, thus, unsustainable. Anybody who is foolish enough to believe in such systems is not only delusional, but will suffer consequences just like any of the aforementioned groups. And since it was leftists, socialists, and liberals who destroyed the United States, turned it into a socialist state, and ruined our futures, the least we can do is enjoy it when they suffer the consequences of their own delusion.

At Least You Know

One of the most painful experiences in my life was switching from a parochial school to a public school in the 7th grade. As my father was a pastor and the school a religious one, I had been thoroughly indoctrinated in Christianity. Since that environment was all I was familiar with in terms of schooling, when I switched to a public school I continued behaving as if I were in a Christian school, not a public one. If somebody cursed I would rat them out. If somebody cheated I would narc on them. And if somebody wore a Motley Crue shirt with its pentagram on it, my Christian schooling told me to lecture the person that it was a symbol of Satan. Naturally this did not ingratiate myself to either the students or the teachers, and I deservedly got the shit kicked out of me every day.

Of course today we can see where I was wrong and why I got daily beatings. But can you imagine what it was like to be a 13 year old kid and not knowing why people hated me? Can you imagine having no clue what you were doing wrong or why the whole school hated you? Can you fathom what it's like to have a kid just punch you for no reason? No parent or older classmate ever sat me down and explained things to me. Nobody told me the reality of the situation. I was left to wander aimlessly and figure it out on my own. It was a miserable existence.

Now imagine that applied to some of your archetypical leftists. Peggy Joseph for example was so delusional she actually believed that Barack Obama was going to pay for her gas and her mortgage. Can you imagine how confused she must be right now? Think of all the youthful idiots who voted for Obama expecting jobs upon graduation. Not only do they not have jobs, they have debts, no hope for a career, and their financial lives are ruined. Can you imagine their confusion? And all the AARP members who thought in voting for socialism their retirements would be guaranteed? Imagine how dumbfounded they're going to be when the checks stop coming. These people are so clueless, so ignorant, so brainwashed about basic economics, they will be condemned to wander aimlessly forever. At least you know why the economy is tanking. At least you know why the checks are no longer coming. Not only will that save your sanity, it will allow you to take action that might remedy the situation.

Forever Envious

Greatness and leftism are mutually exclusive. Since equal-outcomes, fairness, commune, egalitarianism, and conformity are the core principles of most leftist ideologies nothing unique, individualistic, or great will ever come of them. Mediocrity, sameness, dependence, and uniformity are more likely the byproducts of leftist societies.

In theory this shouldn't matter to a leftist. As long as everything is equal in a society, then that society is superior to any other where equality is not achieved. Doesn't matter what their technological advancements are. Doesn't matter how rich their poorest quintile is. Doesn't matter what their GDP per capita is. If that country is not egalitarian, then it is inferior to the leftist utopia. But no matter what leftists tell themselves about equality, none of that overrides their human nature. And it is in their human nature to be envious of greatness.

This is why no matter what happens you will get your revenge in the end, because no leftist or group of leftists will ever repeat the greatness of the United States. No socialist country will even come close to achievements of the United States. The reason is simple. In order to do that, they wouldn't be leftists. They would have to go against their ideology and advocate pro-capitalist and pro-freedom policies. Since this goes against their ideology, and their ideology is more important than anything else, it leaves them with only one option:

Besmirch the United States.

Leftists **hate** the fact the United States has the best track record of any country or any empire in the history of the world. It reminds them of their mediocrity, it reminds them of their commonness, it reminds them of their inferiority to others. But since its track record is unassailable they must criminalize it and vilify it. This is why you have liberal professors constantly trying to re-write history. This is why the United States only achieved its greatness by "stealing it from other countries." This is why the US is nothing but an evil imperialist empire that needs to be destroyed. The left cannot let a successful, capitalist, pro-freedom country stand because it proves they're wrong.

But vilify it all they want, their attempts are in vain. Not just because history will vindicate the United States, but because the United States was based in reality. The United States adhered to the Reality Principle. It put the people first and made the government serve the people. Thusly, any other form of government leftists attempt will not achieve similar success and guarantees the United States will continue to be the envy of all leftists.

Destroyed Gods

As the promises of socialism fail to materialize it will test the individual leftist's loyalty to socialism. If Detroit is any indication this loyalty is strong and unwavering. So strong and unwavering it is damaging to the individual. But loyalty to an ideology can go much deeper than that and has much more serious consequences for the left.

For example, take the Japanese during the final days of WWII. They were so desperate and so committed to Shintoism that they were able to get soldiers and pilots to commit suicide for the emperor. Be it a kamikaze attack or a banzai charge, Japanese soldiers willingly killed themselves and ended their existence for an ideology. Showing even more dedication to their ideology was when Americans started landing on Japan proper, both civilians and soldiers committed suicide rather than be taken prisoner. And trumping that display of fanaticism was when soldiers and civilians needlessly killed themselves *after Japan surrendered* and there was no threat. These people were so dedicated to the emperor and Shintoism that they'd rather die without them (ironically, Emperor Hirohito himself didn't even commit suicide, living until 1989, and Shintoism was never banned, merely separated from the government).

Now most people will point out that Shintoism is a religion while leftism is an ideology, and therefore they are not analogous, but the difference is merely semantic. They're both religions. And liberals and leftists run the same risk as their WWII Shinto counterparts because like their Shinto counterparts they have nothing else to live for.

Understand just how shallow and meaningless your life has to be to the point you take leftism as a religion. I'm not talking about a college student who claims he's a liberal just so he can woo some girl back to his dorm room. I'm talking about the people who are too lazy to achieve anything in life that they believe declaring themselves a "progressive" somehow gives them meaning or worth. People, who when you ask to describe themselves, don't say "I'm a carpenter" or "I'm an accountant," they immediately say "I'm progressive" or "I'm a liberal" because it is core to their being.

If you take their ideology away, what do they have left? The university professor no longer has a point in brainwashing his students. The non-profit volunteer no longer has people dependent upon her. The green-freak no longer derives value on how small his carbon foot print is. And the feminist only has her cats. In the end their lives are meaningless.

This results in an uncomfortable reality for most religious leftists. Since they have nothing besides their politics their entire value is based on their political ideology being proven right, and they will go to great lengths to protect it. This explains why leftists are not only irrational, but they tend to be *very* emotional. If you dare to criticize socialism or leftism they don't view that as a constructive critique of the socialist economic model, they view it as a personal attack on themselves. It also explains why they will probably defend socialism to their grave. Since they have no core, they have no individuality, and they derive their entire value by being a "progressive" or "going green," that ideology has more value than they do as an individual. Therefore they can't possibly be wrong, because if they are, they negate their own reason for existence.

The good news is you don't really have to do anything to exact your toll of revenge in this regard. Yes you can agitate leftists with empirical economic data, making them feel insecure, but in truth all you have to do is sit and watch. Since socialism is not sustainable in the long run, watching reality slowly crush their god will prove to be one of the best ways to enjoy the decline.

Destroyed Lives

I often wonder or theorize about liberals lying on their death bed. For example, say a confirmed feminist is on her death bed. She's always blamed sexism for her problems in life. Always voted democrat. Always thought there was a glass ceiling. She dedicated her entire life to fighting against the patriarch, and in doing so ensured she has no family at her bedside. But before she passes on does she ever ask,

"What if I was wrong? What if men really weren't oppressive, just different? What if I went out with that boy back in college instead of standing him up? Could I have worn heels? Would I have liked family life?"

Alas, the questions are moot as she passes away with those thoughts in her mind.

Along the same lines, say you have a dying black man who has always blamed racism for his problems. He always voted democrat. He always thought he was entitled. And he thought it futile to try. But before he passes on does he ever reflect and ask himself,

"What if I was wrong? What if I tried? What if it wasn't discrimination? And even if it was, would I have lived a better life if I had tried my best? Did I try my best???"

Again, those questions are also moot as he passes away into irrelevance.

The reason I bring these examples up is not out of wishful thinking, but rather to make one very important point. Liberals and leftists, just like everybody else, only get one life. They get one short precious finite life. And when it's over, they're done. They no longer exist. Their one opportunity for consciousness, sentient thought, and self-awareness in the universe is over.

Sadly, most leftists waste this one opportunity.

If you think about human life, though finite, its potential is unlimited. Given a conducive environment, we can do great things, live great lives, and leave a legacy for future generations. So the worst thing that can happen to us is if we somehow get impaired and are no longer capable of achieving our potential. Normally, we think about this in terms of a physical or mental impairment, but we can also be impaired ideologically. And the most debilitating ideological impairment or disease a person can get is leftism.

The sheer potential a human could achieve, only to have a childish, lazy, and naïve ideology like leftism infect them, corrupt them, and prevent them from realizing that potential is the worst thing that could possibly happen to any human being. They have the mental capacity, they have the physical capacity, but they are philosophically impaired, sometimes philosophically paralyzed. And worse, it's self-inflicted.

The consequences of being infect by leftism are life-destroying. Leftism not only infects, but damages every aspect of the host's life. It impairs the host's financial success by making them avoid any sort of challenging subjects.

"Mathematics, engineering, the sciences, all too hard, besides, follow your heart and the money will follow!"

It destroys the hosts ability to find a mate.

"You're sexist for liking skinny girls!" or *"You need a man like you need a bicycle!"*

It decimates the host's family.

"You need a career! You can do it all! You can have it all! We need more government daycare!"

It installs envy, jealousy, even hatred for other people.

"Rich people don't pay their fair share! It's those evil corporations holding us down, man!"

It even installs an auto-immune defense ensuring nobody can treat it or remove it.

"You're just racist/sexist/homophobic/bigoted/misogynist/ignorant/ fascist/close-minded!"

In the end leftism owns the host. It dictates its every move, makes every decision, audits every thought, and ensures the host achieves only a fraction of what it was capable of. It takes the host's one, single, precious, and only life in the universe and makes sure to piss it away. The host never achieves what it could. It never makes any notable contributions to life. And because it's infected with such a warped philosophy, what precious little time it has being conscious is largely spent in a tortured state being angry, confused, disillusioned, and frustrated with the real world.

Sure enough the host will die,

unheard of,

uncared for,

and ultimately irrelevant.

The host's consciousness will have only been proven to be a wasted life.

If there is a revenge for the death of the United States, this is it. If there is payback for leftists ruining your life, this is it. The fact that most leftists and liberals took their one shot at life and chose to ruin it with a defeatist and pessimistic ideology like leftism should provide you the ultimate revenge. While you're making the best of your life, no matter what the challenges, leftists are entirely dependent on the state for their success and happiness. While you're wise enough to appreciate what you have in life, leftists stew away, envying yours. And while you lay there on your death bed, having no regrets because you know you lived the best life you could, the leftist is left there to sit and ponder. It is a revenge so harsh it almost begets pity.

SPONSORS

BUY GLORIOUS HAT!

www.commieobama.com

BANG!

Available at www.rooshv.com

HOW TO SURVIVE LIVING ABROAD

THE EDUCATOR

Available at Amazon!

WORTHLESS

The Young Person's Indispensable Guide to Choosing the Right Major

By

Aaron Clarey

Available on Amazon!

CREDITS

Leslie Eastman of Temple of Mut

Marty Andrade of Martyandrade.wordpress.com

Alicia Stender

Mrs. B of The Lonely Conservative

Veronica Franco

Karen Ziemniak

Chris and Dawn Pohl

Also Special Thanks To

Colin Post of www.expat-chronicles.com
English Teacher X of www.englishteacherx.com
Allie Gadziemski of www.amillionreasons.net
Suzy McCarley
Karl Ushanka of www.commieobama.com
Amber Straub

Made in the USA
Columbia, SC
30 January 2021